WHAT A YEAR IT WAS!
1961

A walk back in time to revisit
what life was like in the year that
has special meaning for you...

*Congratulations
and
Best Wishes*

To

From

DEDICATION

To Melanie — A Most Special, Talented, Loving Lady:

A big "thank you" for being a wonderful wife to my son Lee,
and an incredible mom to my grandchildren, Danielle and Ava.
Happy 40th Birthday
Love,
Bev

Series Created By • Beverly Cohn

Designers • Peter Hess & Marguerite Jones

Research • Laurie Cohn

Special thanks to Kenny Bookbinder for his invaluable help with the sports section

CONTENTS

JFK The New World Leader

The new young president begins the momentous task of guiding the nation through the critical years ahead.

John F. Kennedy is sworn in as the 35th and youngest president of the United States. With ex-presidents **Eisenhower** and **Truman** at the ceremony, and **Herbert Hoover** also living but snowbound, it is the first time since 1885 that three presidents have been alive as the incoming president moves into the White House.

It is a solemn ceremony as he takes the oath of office and assumes the burden laid down by Eisenhower.

"In your hands, my fellow citizens, more than mine, will rest the final success or failure of our course...Now the trumpet summons us again...against the common enemies of man: tyranny, poverty, disease and war itself...And so, my fellow Americans, ask not what your country can do for you, ask what you can do for your country."

WHAT A YEAR IT WAS!

5

PRESIDENT KENNEDY
RESPONDS TO SOVIET THREAT TO SIGN A PEACE TREATY WITH EAST GERMANY

At a press conference, President Kennedy outlines the West's reply to Khrushchev's threats to sign a peace treaty with East Germany:

"A city does not become free merely by calling it a free city. For a city or a people to be free requires they be given the opportunity without economic, political or police pressure to make their own choice and live their own lives. The people of West Berlin today have that freedom. It is the objective of our policy that they will continue to enjoy it. Peace does not come automatically from a quote "peace treaty." There is peace in Germany today even though the situation there is abnormal. A peace treaty that adversely affects the lives and rights of millions will not bring peace with it. A peace treaty that attempts to affect adversely the solemn commitments of three great powers will not bring peace with it. We again urge the Soviet government to reconsider its course, to return to the path of constructive cooperation it so frequently states it desires and to work with its World War II allies in concluding a just and enduring settlement of issues remaining from that conflict."

THE BERLIN WALL

1961

A Tale Of Tragedy

The line of demarcation in the Cold War lies in Berlin with battle-ready Soviet divisions encircling the city while the West deploys 1,000 troops and tanks on the border.

West Berlin, with its burgeoning prosperity, is a thorn in the side of the Reds.

With refugees from the East escaping by the tens of thousands, (below left) **the Communists in desperation close the East-West border and throw up a five-foot concrete wall to seal off the border** (below right).

1961 THE BERLIN WALL

Now entire families are heart-broken as they are separated, their only communication a wave from a distance.

A bride in the East can only wave to her mother in the West following her wedding ceremony.

8

THE BERLIN WALL 1961

Despite a strengthened border the East Germans still attempt escape. This woman hangs from a second story window as Red police try to pull her back but the West Berliners finally succeed in pulling her into freedom.

East Germans grasp any chance to flee. A guard's back is turned, the barbed wire is slashed and Westerners stretch forth willing hands to pull them to asylum. They gamble that a sudden rifle shot won't end their dreams.

The crowd is jubilant as yet another person flees an intolerable way of life.

Freedom is man's most prized possession and this young couple, along with thousands of others, are risking their lives to gain it.

BUILDS MEN

"The **best** to you each morning"

Kellogg's

CORN FLAKES

Kellogg's
CORN
FLAKES

Best liked (*World's favorite*)
Best flavor (*Kellogg's secret*)
Worst to run out of

BIGGEST SOVIET SPY NETWORK SINCE WORLD WAR II UNCOVERED BY BRITISH INTELLIGENCE.

Chou En-lai welcomed to the 22nd Party Congress by Khrushchev.

It is declared at Moscow's 22nd Party Congress that the CIA employs 72,000 spies while the U.S. Department of State estimates that there are 300,000 Soviet-bloc spies.

As part of Khrushchev's de-Stalinization campaign, Stalin's bones are removed from the tomb he shared with Lenin in Moscow's Red Square.

Khrushchev's plan for agricultural decentralization approved by Moscow's Central Committee.

Albania banished from Communist bloc.

✈ **The Soviets return two surviving crewmen of a U.S. Air Force jet shot down in the Barents Sea.**

🎓 **A cultural agreement for the exchange of U.S. and Soviet scholars is signed in Moscow.**

🌐 **The Soviets lift the censorship ban on outgoing news dispatches.**

✌ **Russia proposes a six-month moratorium on the Berlin crisis.**

✈ **The U.S.S.R. and the U.S. agree on direct air service between New York City and Moscow.**

U.S. military train detained by the Soviets for 15 hours on the border between East and West Germany.

Accusing each other of being aggressors, JFK and Khrushchev announce increases in military spending.

Khrushchev and Kennedy meet in Vienna for talks on the future of Berlin.

KENNEDY

KHRUSHCHEV

Mobs take to the streets in **CAIRO** to protest **Patrice Lumumba's** death.

Led by **Moise Tshombe** there is war in **THE CONGO** with that young nation torn apart by civil strife.

CUBA is a trouble spot with **Castro's** Red regime and his boasting that he has always been a Communist.

WORLD IN CRISIS 1961

LAOS
is under the uneasy rule of a neutralist regime.

The **ALGERIAN WAR**
continues to pit brother against brother.

SOUTH VIETNAM
battles Red guerrillas.

1961 AFRICA

THE CONGO

- **African heads of state meet in Casablanca and announce plan for common defense.**

- **18 African nations admitted to the EEC as associates.**

Hassan II

Following the death of his father, Mohammed V, 31-year old Crown Prince Mulay Hassan becomes Hassan II and is new King of Morocco.

- **RWANDA** declares independence from Belgium.

- **NIGERIA** breaks relations with France over continued nuclear tests in the Sahara.

- The U.N. General Assembly condemns 95-1 **SOUTH AFRICA'S** apartheid policies as reprehensible and repugnant to human dignity. The U.S. opposes sanctions against South Africa.

- Former British West African colony of **SIERRA LEONE** becomes an independent nation within the Commonwealth.

- Tom Mboya wins **KENYAN** elections.

The French government restricts the police and political powers of the French army in Algeria.

Algiers seized by French army insurgents.

De Gaulle assumes dictatorial powers in Algeria to crush the mutiny.

Talks with Algerian rebels begin in Evian, France as a 30-day truce is declared.

Presidents Nkrumah (Ghana), Toure (Guinea) and Keita (Mali) sign charter creating a union of African states.

Ghana's Nkrumah takes control of the government and the ruling Convention People's Party.

Former Prime Minister of the Republic of the Congo, **Patrice Lumumba** is transferred from Thysville military prison to a prison in Katanga province.

Patrice Lumumba is assassinated in the Congo.

Proclaiming the end of military rule in the Republic of the Congo, President **Joseph Kasavubu** names a provisional government with **Joseph Ileo** as Prime Minister.

United Arab Republic breaks diplomatic relations with Belgium over the Congo.

Katanga's President **Moise Tshombe** arrested after he walks out of a meeting of Congolese leaders at Coquilhatville.

Moise Tshombe agrees to end his secession from the Congo.

Announcing a $10,000,000 U.N. loan to the Congo, **U.N. Secretary General Dag Hammarskjold** states that the political crisis in the Congo appears to be over.

THE **UNITED** NATIONS IS TORN APART OVER THE **CONGO** ISSUE

In an impassioned speech at the United Nations, **Adlai Stevenson** pleads that *"the only way to keep the Cold War out of the Congo is to keep the United Nations in the Congo...We call on the Soviet Union to join us in thus insuring the free and untrammeled exercise by the Congolese people of their right to independence and to democracy...It is the security of all people which is threatened by the statement and by the proposals of the Soviet government."*

In what appears to be a well-organized protest by members of African nationalist groups in New York, the most violent demonstration by spectators in U.N. history breaks out underscoring the gravity of the Soviet threat.

Hammarskjold

U.N. Secretary General Hammarskjold stands firm, refusing to bow to Communist pressure. His contention that disaster would result if U.N. troops leave the Congo is backed both by **President Kennedy** and by India's **Prime Minister Nehru**.

The riot is put down but the stage is set for a test between the free world and the Communist bloc—the most critical moment in the 15 years of the United Nations existence.

1961

Flags are lowered at the United Nations to pay tribute to DAG HAMMARSKJOLD

The leader of the U.N. is killed in an airplane crash while on a peace mission to the Congo.

A great apostle of peace, he assumed his post in 1953 and brought to his work a dedication that won him international respect even from the Russians who, even though they tried to remove him, never questioned his integrity.

U Thant of Burma is sworn in to succeed Mr. Hammarskjold in guiding the U.N. through the perilous times it faces.

WHAT A YEAR IT WAS!

1961 ADVERTISEMENT

GOOD COFFEE IS LIKE FRIENDSHIP: RICH AND WARM AND STRONG

Coffee is the life of the party.
Nothing else comes close.
So make it extra-good every time: dark-rich and rewarding.
With a heaping tablespoon of coffee
for every friendly cup.

MAKE IT COFFEE. MAKE IT OFTEN. MAKE IT RIGHT.

Pan-American Coffee Bureau, 120 Wall Street, N.Y. 5, N.Y.

17

1961

Ernesto "Che" Guevara,

National Bank President, is sworn in as Cuba's head of the Ministry of Industry.

★

The U.S. Embassy staff in Havana ordered reduced to 11 people within 48 hours by Fidel Castro.

★

Washington breaks diplomatic relations with Cuba.

★

Castro ends free elections in Cuba making it a socialist country.

★ Havana

CUBA

Fidel Castro

THE BAY OF PIGS TRAGEDY

• Over 1,400 CIA-trained anti-Castro Cuban exiles invade their homeland in a failed attempt to overthrow the Castro government. Equipped by the U.S., over 400 die at the Bay of Pigs during the three-day battle when U.S. air support fails to materialize.

• Castro strikes rebels on the beach with MIG's and tanks. JFK warns the Soviets.

• President Kennedy issues a statement taking full responsibility for the fiasco.

• After conferring with President Kennedy at Camp David, Eisenhower expresses support for JFK.

• Castro says 500 U.S. bulldozers is the exchange price for 1,217 rebels captured in the Bay of Pigs invasion.

• President Kennedy makes an appeal to U.S. citizens to donate tractors to the Tractors for Freedom committee for the release of imprisoned Cuban rebels.

• The tractors-for-prisoners exchange talks collapse between the U.S. and Cuba.

• Cuba challenges U.S. right to retain Guantanamo Bay Naval Base.

In Rio de Janeiro, Brazil and the U.S. sign their first extradition treaty.

Dominican Republic dictator Rafael Trujillo assassinated as he leaves his home in San Cristobal ending a 31-year rule.

✈ An armed passenger seizes a U.S. airliner en route from Miami to Tampa and forces it to fly to Havana.

✈ Following the hijacking and recapture of a U.S. commercial jet in Texas, the U.S. Federal Aviation Agency authorizes U.S. airlines to arm their crews on all flights.

✈ Cuba releases Pan American jet hijacked over Mexico.

✈ The Federal Aviation Act of 1958 is amended making hijacking an airliner a federal offense punishable by death and authorizes federal penalties for other crimes committed on a commercial aircraft.

WHAT A YEAR IT WAS!

EUROPE

✺ France's President **CHARLES DE GAULLE** receives endorsement from three out of four French voters in a national referendum on his policy for Algerian administrative reforms and self-determination.

✺ France's President de Gaulle target of assassination attempt as he drives from Paris to his home at Colombey-les-Deux-Eglises.

✺ **England's EDWARD HEATH begins negotiations for British entry into the European Common Market.**

✺ **In London, Parliament approves joining the European Common Market.**

Following the tradition of non-alignment, SWEDEN refuses to join the EEC.

✺ Henri Manoury arrested in de Gaulle murder plot.

Charles de Gaulle

Poland's **Bohdan Winiarski** is elected president of the 15-member International Court of Justice.

Conrad Adenauer reelected for his fourth successive term as chancellor of West Berlin.

West Germany launches its first submarine since World War II.

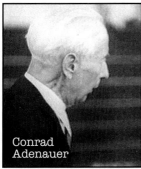

Conrad Adenauer

Spain's Generalissimo Francisco Franco denounces Western policy, capitalism and democracy.

Marshal Tito

Yugoslavia's TITO holds conference in Belgrade with 25 neutral nations.

WHAT A YEAR IT WAS!

China

Vietnam

Laos

Cambodia

Laos

☆ To end the civil war, the Laotian government announces it is willing to accept a policy of neutrality. Pro-Communist forces launch a major offensive in central Laos.

☆ U.S. calls on non-Communist nations to join in efforts to support and maintain independence of Laos.

☆ **British Prime Minister Macmillan** meets with **President Kennedy** in Washington to discuss increased Communist activities in Laos.

☆ A joint appeal to the Soviets to meet proposals for ending the fighting in Laos is issued in Key West, Florida by **Kennedy** and **Macmillan**.

☆ Moscow joins the U.S. in seeking a cease-fire in Laos.

☆ Cease-fire becomes effective in Laos on all fronts.

☆ International conference on Laos opens in Geneva with 14 nations participating.

☆ The Communists are accused of a "cynical disregard" of the cease-fire in Laos by the U.S. delegation in Geneva.

Vietnam

☆ According to reports out of Saigon, Viet Cong are killing 200-250 people a month.

☆ **Vice President Lyndon B. Johnson** arrives in Saigon on an official tour of South and Southeast Asia. He announces a $40 million increase in U.S. military and economic aid.

☆ **Kennedy** sends another 200 American military advisors into Vietnam.

☆ With 78% of the total vote, South Vietnam's **President Ngo Dinh Diem** is swept back into office.

☆ **Diem** declares Vietnam is now engaged in a real war not a guerrilla war.

☆ **James Davis** is the first American slain by Viet Cong troops in Vietnam.

WHAT A YEAR IT WAS!

Is your house better insured than you are?

According to U.S. Government figures, the average man with a high school education will earn $243,000 during his lifetime.

Think of what this money will buy over the years. Food. Clothing. A house. Medical care. Education for the children. Then ask yourself: how much of all these same things would your present life insurance buy?

$10,000 life insurance is not enough

for a man who's worth what you are.

A trained John Hancock agent can show you a number of ways to increase your life insurance so that it will more reasonably reflect your real worth to your family.

One way: for as little as $3 a week a young father can guarantee his widow an added income of $100 a month until his present children are of age.

When your John Hancock agent calls, ask him how you can give your family maximum financial protection against the loss of their most valuable property—*you.*

John Hancock

MUTUAL LIFE INSURANCE COMPANY
BOSTON, MASSACHUSETTS

21

A MAN WHOSE NAME IS WRITTEN IN INFAMY

Spectators, many of whom are concentration camp survivors, fill an Israeli courtroom and relive their personal horror as Adolf Eichmann is tried for his crimes against humanity.

Found guilty on 15 counts, Eichmann sits emotionless in a bulletproof booth as the charges are summed up.

During the four-month trial, the three judges have been studying the evidence against Eichmann who was seized in Buenos Aires last year and taken to Israel. The unseen witnesses against the former Gestapo colonel are the six million Jews he is convicted of slaughtering.

Justice is finally served as the man who escaped the Nuremberg war trials by fleeing to South America stands to receive his death sentence from the very people whom he tried to wipe out.

WHAT A YEAR IT WAS!

NEAR EAST

Ben-Gurion

Despite receiving a 77-26 vote of confidence by the Knesset the day before, **Israeli Prime Minister David Ben-Gurion** resigns because of his unpopular refusal to absolve Pinhas Lavon of spy charges even though he is found innocent by a special investigatory committee.

United Arab Republic accuses the Soviets of imperialistic motives in the Arab world.

Syria rebels and severs political ties to Egypt. Nasser formally gives up claims to Syria.

Turkey abolishes ban on opposition parties.

Convicted of violating his country's constitution and other crimes, Turkey's former premier **Adnan Menderes** is hanged.

British troops land in **Kuwait** to defend against possible Iraqi invasion.

Great Britain gives up protectorate over oil-rich Kuwait but commits to continuing military aid.

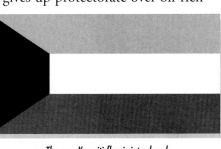

The new Kuwaiti flag is introduced.

WHAT A YEAR IT WAS!

ASIA

South Korea

North Korea

834 newspapers and news agencies are outlawed in South Korea for "improper registration" and 25 businessmen and officials are arrested by the government for corrupt activities.

A 10-year military aid pact with North Korea is signed in Moscow.

BURMA becomes world's first Buddhist republic.

Over protests by Tamil-speaking Hindus, Sinhalese replaces English as Ceylon's official language.

Nepal's King Mahendra orders restoration of civil rights suspended since December of last year.

Nepal settles its border dispute with Communist China.

Following Senate confirmation, **President Kennedy's** cabinet nominees are sworn in:

Secretary of State:	**Dean Rusk**
Secretary of the Treasury:	**C. Douglas Dillon**
Secretary of Defense:	**Robert S. McNamara**
Attorney General:	**Robert F. Kennedy**
Postmaster General:	**J. Edward Day**
Secretary of the Interior:	**Stewart L. Udall**
Secretary of Agriculture:	**Orville L. Freeman**
Secretary of Commerce:	**Luther H. Hodges**
Secretary of Labor:	**Arthur J. Goldberg**
Secretary of Health, Education & Welfare:	**Abraham A. Ribicoff**
Chief Delegate to U.N.:	**Adlai E. Stevenson**

- *A new cabinet position on housing and urban development* is recommended by President Kennedy's special task force appointed to study housing.

- *President Kennedy creates the U.S. Government Ethics Committee* chaired by **Judge Calvert Magruder** to study the ethical standards of all government agencies.

- *Edward R. Murrow* appointed director of the U.S. Information Agency.

- *President Kennedy* abolishes 17 U.S. interdepartmental advisory and policy-making committees set up under former **President Eisenhower**.

- *President Kennedy goes on a state visit to London* to confer with **Prime Minister Macmillan**.

- *President Kennedy* extends U.S. Civil Rights Commission.

WHAT A YEAR IT WAS!

I n his farewell speech to the nation after eight years in office and 50 years of public service, President **Dwight D. Eisenhower** warns the nation against a growing *"military-industrial complex"* and that *"the potential for the disastrous rise of misplaced power exists and will persist."* He also foresees the possibility of public policy becoming *"the captive of a scientific-technological elite."*

FAMOUS
George Stephanopoulos
BIRTH

President Kennedy signs a bill restoring Five-Star Rank to former President Eisenhower.

Ultra-conservative group, the **John Birch Society**, is criticized by the U.S. Congress for alleged accusations of Communist leanings leveled against former President Eisenhower and other high-ranking officials.

• • • • • • • • • • • • • •

Democrat from Texas **Sam Rayburn** elected to his 10th term as Speaker of the House at the first session of the 87th U.S. Congress.

SAM RAYBURN

• • • • • • • • • • • • • •

The 23rd Amendment to the Constitution grants Washington D.C. residents the right to vote in presidential elections.

• • • • • • • • • • • • • •

President Kennedy names 37-year old Harvard professor **Henry Kissinger** part-time consultant on national security affairs.

• • • • • • • • • • • • • •

U.S. Agency for International Development created under the Foreign Assistance Act.

Paul-Henri Spaak resigns as Secretary General of NATO.

Thomas K. Finletter is named permanent U.S. representative to NATO by President Kennedy.

NATO

UNITED NATIONS

Over U.S. protests, the U.N. adopts ban on nuclear arms.

In a victory for the U.S., the United Nations denies a seat to Peking.

PASSINGS

A member of Congress since 1913 and Speaker of the House for 17 years, **SAM RAYBURN** dies at age 79 from cancer. President Kennedy, ex-Presidents Truman and Eisenhower and protégè Vice President Lyndon B. Johnson attend the funeral for the man who served under eight presidents and worked his way through college by sweeping floors and ringing the bell for classes.

One of the fairest and most respected judges to ever sit on the bench, **JUDGE LEARNED HAND** dies at age 89.

WHAT A YEAR IT WAS!

Queen Elizabeth In India

Queen Elizabeth rides with President Prasad

to the reviewing stand in New Delhi where Prime Minister Nehru greets the royal party.

In addition to visiting India, Her Majesty's tour will include Pakistan, Persia, Cyprus and Ghana.

Some three million people watch the mammoth procession.

WHAT A YEAR IT WAS!

During The Nation's 11th Anniversary
Celebration Of Independence

Modern India recalls the colorful days of Empire. Republic Day presents a dazzling panorama of India's many races in the gala parade.

The Air Force is represented by this float *(right)*.

Spectators watch the highlight of the parade, the traditional elephants recalling days of Mogul grandeur *(right)*.

IF IT'S

RICHFIELD

IT'S RIGHT FOR YOUR CAR

A normal car's abnormal life...

"Four stop lights to the football field; three right turns and a left for groceries; stop and start on the way to work." It sounds normal, and it is—for the people, but not necessarily for the family car.

Richfield men understand that this kind of "normal" driving is harder on your car than pleasure trips on the open road. That's why they use special equipment for proper lubrication, recommend protective oil changes, assist you in the use of products *right* for your car.

As right as NEW Richfield Boron, the over-100-octane gasoline that's *2 ways new...10 ways better* to protect your car's engine—to stretch your driving dollars.

NEW Richfield Boron contains a remarkable new carburetor-cleaning additive that practically ends forever the need for costly carburetor "boil-outs." It effectively cleans out carburetor deposits *as you drive*...and then *keeps* your carburetor clean and clear of *future* deposits.

Make all your service stops Richfield stops. Discover the years-ahead quality that is built into every Richfield product and service. Quality created with one idea in mind: Make it *right* for *your* car.

RICHFIELD

SYMBOL OF QUALITY TO WESTERN MOTORISTS

People

1961

Jack & Jackie's First Christmas In The White House

The President and First Lady stand in front of the White House Christmas tree decorated with Tchaikovsky's *Nutcracker Suite* as its theme.

The Christmas season brings Mrs. Kennedy to a children's hospital in Washington for a visit with ill and crippled children.

Mrs. Kennedy passes from ward to ward with a little token for each child. The gracious lady finds most a little shy but none shy enough to refuse her gift.

The First Lady makes the visit to bring a little cheer to the unfortunate tots who will spend the holidays in the hospital.

A glimpse into the busy life of the First Lady.

Kennedys

In the first TV interview granted by **Jackie Kennedy**, the First Lady expresses her concern over the excessive spotlight placed on **Caroline** and worries about the future effect it could have on her young daughter.

• **Rose Kennedy**, mother of JFK, releases a letter the President wrote as a young boy to his father wherein he pleads for a raise in his allowance from $ .40 to $ .70 weekly.

• **President Kennedy** will soon ride in a custom-built Lincoln Continental complete with a removable bubble top and an electrically adjustable backseat so that even short dignitaries can be raised to viewable proportions.

Left, Right And Center

In a gesture to accommodate the visiting American president, Britain alters its tradition of driving on the left side of the road and allows JFK to drive on the right.

Jackeee, Oui

First Lady **Jacqueline Kennedy**, who receives an estimated 500 letters a day, sets a new precedent answering some of her mail in French with the help of her French secretary.

Jackie Enchants The French

Over a million French people line the streets of Paris to get a peek at the beautiful American First Lady who is accompanying her husband on his trip to meet with **President de Gaulle**. Later at a press luncheon for 400 journalists **President Kennedy** quips: *"I do not feel it inappropriate for me to introduce myself. I am the man who accompanied Jacqueline Kennedy to Paris."*

• **The Kennedys** receive a wonderful welcome upon their arrival in San Juan, Puerto Rico, the first leg of their weekend trip to Venezuela and Colombia.

• America's First Lady **Jackie Kennedy** dazzles the Greeks on her vacation visit to Athens and the Aegean Islands.

WHAT A YEAR IT WAS!

They'll Do It His Way

Frank Sinatra and **Peter Lawford** fly into Washington on President-elect **John F. Kennedy's** Convair, the *Caroline*, to plan Inauguration Eve's entertainment which will include appearances by **Mahalia Jackson, Milton Berle, Ethel Merman, Juliet Prowse, Sir Laurence Olivier, Jimmy Durante** and conductor **Leonard Bernstein**.

Sinatra

Durante

Olivier

WHAT A YEAR IT WAS!

Helen Keller
Visits The White House

$\mathcal{A}$t the White House **President Kennedy** receives **Helen Keller**, deaf and blind since childhood.

$\mathcal{M}$iss Keller's hands, tapped in the finger code by her companion, Evelyn Side, provides her with understanding of the world around her.

$\mathcal{M}$iss Keller's life has made her a symbol of hope and achievement for the handicapped. In her remarkable career, she has met every president since Grover Cleveland. Now eighty years of age, alert and vigorous, Helen Keller continues with her inspiring way.

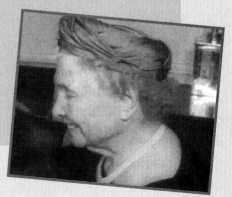

SIR WINSTON CHURCHILL
Celebrates His 87th Birthday

Photographers and well-wishers gather around the Hyde Park Gate home of Sir Winston Churchill to pay tribute to the man who stands among the greatest in British history.

People arrive with gifts for Britain's elder statesman who symbolized the strength and courage of a war-torn country.

His pace may have slowed but indomitable as ever, he prepares to go to the House of Commons for a bipartisan tribute. The man who led his people through some of their darkest days, Mr. Churchill will live in the hearts of free people as one of the great men of our age.

Sir Winston and Lady Churchill leave for the House of Commons.

1961 ADVERTISEMENT

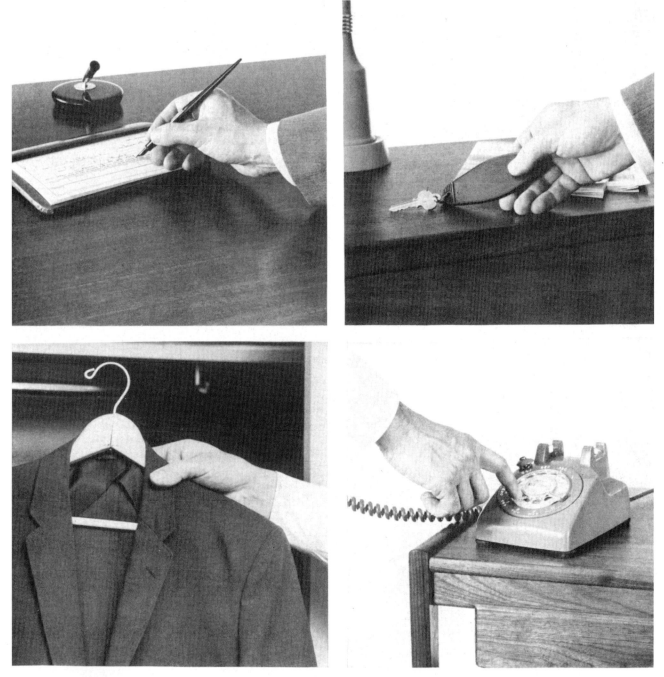

...then, check in at home by Long Distance!

It's the *personal* way to find out your wife and children are well ...to tell them about your trip.

LONG DISTANCE RATES ARE LOW
Here are some examples:

Charleston, W. Va. to Pittsburgh	55¢
Milwaukee to Minneapolis	70¢
Newark, N. J. to Cleveland	85¢
Boston to Chicago	$1.20
Seattle to Washington, D. C.	$1.75

These are the Station-to-Station rates for the first three minutes, after 6 p.m. and all day Sunday. Add the 10% federal excise tax.

Keep in touch by Long Distance... **BELL TELEPHONE SYSTEM**

33

1961

POOL-PLAYING MAMA

Queen Mother Elizabeth becomes the first woman ever served a drink in the all-male London Press Club's smoky bar where she impresses the members with her sharp billiard skills.

- **Queen Elizabeth II** and **Prince Philip** receive a private audience with **Pope John XXIII**.
- **Queen Elizabeth II** bestows the title of Earl of Snowdon on her sister **Margaret's** husband, **Antony Armstrong-Jones**.
- **Princess Margaret** gives birth to **Viscount Linley**, fifth in line to the throne.

CRUMPETS & CAVIAR

Russian cosmonaut Yuri Gagarin lunches with Queen Elizabeth II and Prince Philip at Buckingham Palace.

ENDING ON A HIGH NOTE

For the first time in its history, Milan's La Scala opera house puts on a private performance. England's visiting Queen Elizabeth II and Prince Philip are presented a 12-minute excerpt from Donizetti's *Lucia di Lammermoor* with Australian soprano Joan Sutherland singing Lucia.

Jordan's **King Hussein** marries Antoinette Gardiner, daughter of a British army officer, in Amman.

Yielding right of succession to the Norwegian throne, **Princess Astrid** marries a commoner in Oslo.

AMAZING GRACE

Dressed in a Kelly green outfit, PRINCESS GRACE of Monaco dazzles the Irish as she accompanies husband PRINCE RAINIER on a visit to Dublin on the first official royal visit in the history of the Irish Republic.

On Monaco's National Day, Princess Grace, Princess Caroline (4) and Prince Albert (3) watch a military parade commemorating the twelfth anniversary of Prince Rainier's installation.

A LUNCHEON FIT FOR THE ROYALS

Monaco's Prince Rainier and Princess Grace dine at the White House with President Kennedy.

The Emperor Takes A House

Japanese Emperor Hirohito is preparing to move with his family into a new home that will serve as the Imperial household.

A combination of modern and traditional Japanese styles, the house is the epitome of comfort without being palatial.

The Western influence has invaded the palace grounds, for there's a barbecue pit in the garden and air-conditioning, television and hi-fi in the house.

By coincidence, moving day for the man who was once called the "son of heaven" comes on the 20th anniversary of Pearl Harbor.

HOW WILL HE HANDLE THIS WOMAN?

At an auction held in the home of the Italian Ambassador to the U.N. **EGIDIO ORTONA** to benefit **GIAN-CARLO MENOTTI'S** Festival of Two Worlds in Spoleto, auctioneer **LEONARD BERNSTEIN** bangs his gavel down at $350 for the sale of **RICHARD BURTON** to **ELSA MAXWELL**.

Bernstein

TAKING IT SITTING DOWN

90-year old financier and philanthropist **BERNARD BARUCH**, who is known for enjoying sitting on park benches, donates $30,000 for the building of a park on Manhattan's crowded Lower East Side with lots of, you guessed it, benches.

The search ends for the 23-year old son of New York **Governor & Mrs. Nelson A. Rockefeller**, reported missing at sea in a small native boat off the coast of New Guinea.

Greta Garbo returns to her native Sweden for the first time in 13 years and still wants to be alone.

AN EXPLOSIVE EXPERIENCE

Hollywood dancer **Gene Kelly**, in Paris to direct **Jackie Gleason** in "Gigot," experiences France's right-wing terrorism as fragments from a bomb aimed at a police station land on his car.

FRANKLY, THAT REPORTER DIDN'T GIVE A DAMN

When asked by a reporter at New York's Idlewild airport what role she played in "Gone With the Wind," the aging **Vivien Leigh** (Scarlett O'Hara) storms off in a huff threatening to return to England immediately and not continue on to Atlanta for a revival showing of the 1939 classic film.

DON'T MESS WITH ZSA ZSA DAHLING

Zsa Zsa Gabor files a $6 million lawsuit against Fawcett Publications for defamation of character for depicting her as a gold digger with very little acting ability.

Bobby-sox idol **Fabian** doesn't get to graduate with his classmates from South Philadelphia High School as he lacks the necessary credits in English and mathematics.

Bette Davis (53) takes time out of her Broadway rehearsals of "The Night of the Iguana" to slap a $1 million libel suit against Dell Publishing who characterize the actress as being morose, pathetic, grotesque and ridiculous.

Sir Winston Churchill's pony High Hat, a 5-to-4 favorite, wins the Winston Churchill Stakes at London's Hurst Park.

RICHARD NIXON

writes his first newspaper column, syndicated by *The Los Angeles Times-Mirror*.

Former NAACP attorney **THURGOOD MARSHALL** is sworn in as a judge in the United States Second Circuit Court of Appeals, becoming only the second black to hold this high-level judgeship.

WHAT A YEAR IT WAS!

Rewarding Experiences

Jack Benny is honored in his hometown of Waukegan, Illinois with the dedication of a new school — *Jack Benny Junior High School*.

*F*or his outstanding contribution to the cause of freedom, West Berlin Mayor **Willy Brandt** receives Freedom House's Freedom Award.

*N*otre Dame's Laetare Medal for the outstanding American Roman Catholic layman of the year goes to **President John F. Kennedy**.

*V*ice President Lyndon B. Johnson's 17-year old daughter **Lynda** is crowned the Azalea Queen at the eighth International Azalea Festival in Norfolk, Virginia.

*M*argaret Sanger, unrelenting crusader for planned parenthood, is honored by leaders of a world population crisis conference for her "prophetic vision" 45 years after she opened her first birth control clinic in Brooklyn, New York.

*F*or distinguished service in the cause of freedom, AFL-CIO president **George Meany** receives the Four Freedoms Foundation's Tenth Annual Award.

Nobel Peace Prize
•
Dag Hammarskjold
Sweden

The U.S. Senate introduces a bill calling for a $2,500 gold medal for *Bob Hope* for his 20 years of entertaining troops around the world.

AND THEN THERE WERE NONE
Despite protests of two Exeter University students, best-selling mystery author **Agatha Christie** receives an honorary doctor of letters degree from the famed English university.

• German-born missile expert **Dr. Wernher von Braun** is named "1961 International Boss of the Year" by the International Secretaries Association.

• Instrumental in the creation of the first atomic sub, crusty **Vice-Admiral Hyman G. Rickover** receives the Navy's Distinguished Service Medal.

• French undersea explorer **Captain Jacques-Yves Cousteau** receives the National Geographic Society Gold Medal which is presented to him by President Kennedy.

• President Kennedy presents the Distinguished Service Medal of the National Aeronautics and Space Administration to **Alan Shepard, Jr.**, the nation's symbol of courage.

THE BEST FATHER OF THEM ALL
U.S. Permanent Representative to the U.N. **Adlai Stevenson** is named "Father of the Year" by the National Father's Day Committee.

ON HIS HONOR HE WILL TRY
John F. Kennedy, the first American president to be in scouting as a youngster, is named honorary president of the Boy Scouts of America.

For his contribution to better race relations, former President Harry S. Truman receives the Carver Award from the George Washington Carver Memorial Institute.

During an acceptance speech at the University of Louisville where he receives an honorary degree, former President Truman verbally attacks the John Birch Society calling them worse than the Ku Klux Klan.

What's got into Tang?

NEW NEW NEW

INSTANT
Tang
BREAKFAST
DRINK

More Vitamins C and A

A NEW BOLDER TASTE

Nothing bashful about the new taste of TANG. Make it by the decanterful, serve it ice cold. It's a fact: the colder the TANG, the bolder the taste of TANG. And TANG doesn't lose any of its vitamin C when stored in your refrigerator overnight. When thirst can't wait, make instant TANG a refreshing glass at a time. Remember, use ice cold water for that nice bold taste. *More vitamin C than orange juice*. And the vitamin content *never varies*. Drink TANG for breakfast, and get *extra* vitamin C you need for extra health protection.

GENERAL FOODS KITCHENS

MORE VITALITY VITAMIN C THAN ORANGE JUICE Another fine product from General Foods Kitchens

COHEN

COSTELLO

SINGING UP THE RIVER

After being denied an opportunity to sing before being sentenced for 10 counts of contempt of Congress because of his refusal to tell the House Un-American Activities Committee about his possible Communist affiliations, banjo-playing folk-singer **Pete Seeger** is sentenced to a year in prison.

- Former child star **Jackie Coogan** is arraigned in Calabasas, CA on a drunk driving charge.

- **Al Pacino** is arrested for carrying a concealed weapon.

- Gaining the respect of the other 24 district attorneys, $1 a year Suffolk County, Massachusetts Assistant District Attorney **Edward M. "Ted" Kennedy** obtains his first major conviction against an accomplice in an attempted holdup of a liquor store.

- Kenyan nationalist **Jomo Kenyatta** is free after spending nine years in prison for leading the Mau-Mau rebellion.

- **Mildred Gillars**, known as **Axis Sally**, is paroled from a U.S. prison after serving 12 years of a 10-30 term for treason for broadcasting Nazi propaganda to Allied troops during World War II.

- After being locked up in a Chinese prison for 10 years, American **Robert McCann** is released.

CRAPPED OUT

Ex-gambler **MICKEY COHEN** is convicted in Los Angeles on eight counts of income tax evasion from 1945-1950 to the tune of $347,669 and is sentenced to 15 years in prison and fined $30,000.

HE TOOK A GAMBLE, AND LOST

Gangster **FRANK COSTELLO** loses his U.S. Supreme Court appeal to retain his citizenship.

ALL IN THE FAMILY

AL CAPONE'S older brother, **RALPH**, is hauled into Chicago's Federal Court for $217,716 in income tax evasion dating back to before 1935 when he was billed for $87,217.33.

WHAT ARE YOU, SOME KIND OF SPACE CADET?

Doing 30 in a 45 mph stretch of Florida's U.S. 1 on their way to the dog races, astronauts **Virgil I. "Gus" Grissom** and **Alan Shepard, Jr.** are stopped by a traffic officer who gives Mr. Grissom a warning to "restrict his speed to straight up."

A Whole Lot Of Missing Payments Goin' On

Testifying that he has insufficient funds to pay overdue child support, rock 'n' roll singer **Jerry Lee Lewis** is found guilty of contempt of court and ordered to pay $700.

Don't Steal His Blue Suede Shoes

After ringing his doorbell and not getting an answer, two 14-year old girls break into **Elvis Presley's** Bel-Air home and help themselves to some souvenirs including a few sweaters, photographs and records which are promptly returned by the girls' parents.

WHAT A YEAR IT WAS!

1961

Coupling

Larry King & Alene Akins

Peter Fonda & Susan Brewer

Lauren Bacall & Jason Robards, Jr.

Petula Clark & Claude Wolff

Aretha Franklin & Ted White

Lee Majors & Kathy Robinson

Richard Benjamin & Paula Prentiss

Arthur Miller & Ingeborg Morath

Dennis Hopper & Brooke Hayward

Lucille Ball & Gary Morton

Audrey Meadows & Robert Six

Geraldine Page & Rip Torn

Martin Sheen & Janet Templeton

Ben Gazzara & Janice Rule

Ginger Rogers & William Marshall

Vivian Vance & John Dodds

David Nelson & June Blair

Jack Nicholson & Sandra Knight

Marvin Gaye & Anna Ruby Gordy

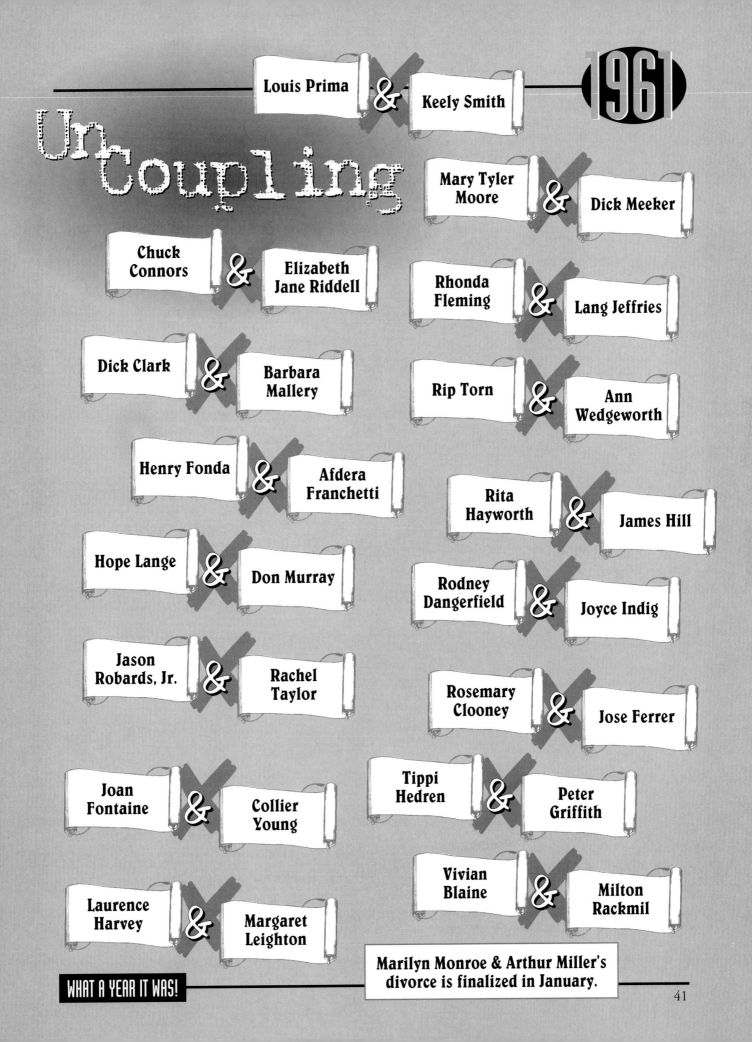

UnCoupling

Louis Prima & Keely Smith

Mary Tyler Moore & Dick Meeker

Chuck Connors & Elizabeth Jane Riddell

Rhonda Fleming & Lang Jeffries

Dick Clark & Barbara Mallery

Rip Torn & Ann Wedgeworth

Henry Fonda & Afdera Franchetti

Rita Hayworth & James Hill

Hope Lange & Don Murray

Rodney Dangerfield & Joyce Indig

Jason Robards, Jr. & Rachel Taylor

Rosemary Clooney & Jose Ferrer

Joan Fontaine & Collier Young

Tippi Hedren & Peter Griffith

Laurence Harvey & Margaret Leighton

Vivian Blaine & Milton Rackmil

Marilyn Monroe & Arthur Miller's divorce is finalized in January.

WHAT A YEAR IT WAS!

41

1961 GENERAL

FEELING THE PAIN AND DOING IT ANYWAY

Despite severe back pain sustained at a tree planting ceremony in Ottawa, Canada and his press secretary Pierre Salinger's announcement that President Kennedy would appear at a press conference on crutches, JFK appears without crutches.

- An announcement from the White House reveals that President Kennedy is suffering from a strained back.

- President Kennedy flies to Palm Beach, Florida to be near his father, Joseph P. Kennedy, who suffered a stroke.

- To ease President Kennedy's back pain, Dr. Janet Travell prescribes a rocking chair for his White House office.

- President Kennedy given a clean bill of health following his physical exam.

Former President Dwight D. Eisenhower is resting in his Palm Springs, California home unable to play golf due to a lumbago attack.

Marilyn Maladies:

With advice from her doctors to avoid fats and fried foods for the rest of her life, Marilyn Monroe leaves New York's Polyclinic Hospital after gallbladder surgery.

- Marilyn checks into the Payne Whitney Psychiatric Clinic of New York Hospital-Cornell Medical Center for mental strain brought on by an intense year of shooting two films back to back and marital problems.

- Following her confinement, Marilyn joins her friend and ex-husband Joe DiMaggio in Redington Beach, Florida to recuperate.

- Marilyn has minor gynecological surgery.

The patient by the name of *George Saviers* who checked into the Mayo Clinic in Rochester, Minnesota for high blood pressure turns out to be the old man of the sea, 61-year old author ERNEST HEMINGWAY.

Billy Graham loses his voice as he recovers from a bronchial infection.

42

HOSPITAL

JUNE ALLYSON is recovering in Santa Monica, California after the removal of polyps from her vocal cords.

✚ Actress **ANN SOTHERN** and her 16-year old daughter are being treated for minor cuts and bruises sustained in a car accident while the daughter was driving on U.S. 101.

✚ Comedian **MEL BLANC** is recovering at UCLA Medical Center after sustaining head injuries and compound fractures of both legs in a head-on collision on Sunset Boulevard.

✚ **RANDOLPH SCOTT** is recovering from hernia surgery at the Mayo Clinic.

✚ **CHERYL CRANE**, 17-year old daughter of Hollywood screen star **LANA TURNER**, is committed to a psychiatric hospital in Hartford, Connecticut.

✚ In London filming *Cleopatra*, **ELIZABETH TAYLOR**'s condition is described as grave when she is struck down with a severe case of pneumonia necessitating a tracheotomy to assist her in breathing.

J.G. TRAVELL, a pain specialist, is the first female physician to be appointed personal doctor to a sitting president and is the first non-military physician since the Harding administration.

Princess Margaret has to stay close to the castle to nurse a bout with influenza.

a RoYaL pain in The you Know What

An announcement comes from Kensington Palace that the Duchess of Kent, the Queen's aunt, is confined to bed with a case of the flu.

Nursing a cracked bone in her left foot, Britain's Queen Mother Elizabeth christens the new $20 million liner "Northern Star" from a wheelchair.

THE PRINCE SEES SPOTS

Buckingham Palace announces that **PRINCE CHARLES**, 12-year old heir to the throne, has the measles and is in Cheam School infirmary.

Returning from Laos, jungle physician **THOMAS DOOLEY (33)** is hospitalized in Manhattan for a recurring bout with cancer which began in 1959 and succumbs to the disease.

While heading an expedition on Mount Makalu in the Himalayas, conqueror of Mount Everest, 41-year old Sir Edmund Hillary, suffers a mild stroke.

1961 — let's celebrate

63-year old Borscht Belt comedian **GEORGE JESSEL** announces he will retire next year and live on the French Riviera.

Former President Dwight D. Eisenhower, now a private citizen, becomes a nine-to-fiver as he begins working at his new office on the campus of Gettysburg College.

ROLLIN' ROLLIN' ROLLIN' HE KEEPS ON ROLLIN'

Rhode Island's Democratic senator Theodore Francis Greene retires at 93 after 24 years in the Senate, holding the distinction of being the oldest man ever to serve in the Senate.

WHAT'S A 42 YEAR DIFFERENCE ANYWAY?

79-year old PABLO PICASSO marries his 37-year old model Jacqueline Roque.

- Arriving in Manila to participate in the 15th anniversary celebration of Filipino independence, 81-year old General Douglas MacArthur receives a very enthusiastic welcome and tells the crowd at the airport: "I have returned."

- In Manhattan, General Douglas MacArthur celebrates his 81st birthday at a stag dinner thrown at the 14th annual reunion of the senior officers of his World War II Southwest Pacific Area Command.

famous births......

PRINCESS Diana

Fabio

Actress Joanne Woodward and her husband-actor Paul Newman have their second child – a girl.

Mrs. Kay Gable, widow of the late film actor Clark Gable who died of a heart attack last November, gives birth to their 8-pound son who is named John Clark.

Humphrey Bogart's widow, Lauren Bacall, (37) gives birth to the first child with her new husband, Jason Robards, Jr. (39) in New York City.

Sammy Davis, Jr., and his Swedish actress-wife May Britt have their first child – a 7-pound, 7-ounce daughter.

WHAT A YEAR IT WAS!

let's celebrate 1961

HAPPY BIRTHDAY JUDGE

Chief Justice of the Supreme Court Earl Warren celebrates his 70th birthday in Washington, D.C.

ELEANOR ROOSEVELT

celebrates her 77th birthday working, getting her hair done and taking tea at home with her family and friends.

A HUMANITARIAN ◘ CELEBRATES ◘◘◘ HER ◘◘◘ BIRTHDAY

HELEN KELLER celebrates her 81st birthday at the home of Katharine Cornell on Martha's Vineyard.

● In celebration of his first birthday, boasting a vocabulary of "Da-da," "Ma-ma" and a variety of other sounds, John F. Kennedy, Jr. gets his first post-christening portrait which shows him chewing on a toy.

● Among the gifts Caroline Kennedy receives for her fourth birthday is a miniature guitar.

No Hole-In-One Here

Vacationing near the Mid-Ocean Club golf course in Bermuda, former President Harry S. Truman quips that he would not be playing golf as he's "never had the money or the skill for it."

1961

IT'S NO SECRET ANYMORE

Hey Buddy, Do You Have Change For A Quarter?

Tired of people using his phone without permission, billionaire oilman J. Paul Getty installs a pay phone in his lavish Tudor mansion outside London.

U.S. Secret Service uncovers a plot by pro-Castro Cubans in Palm Beach, Florida to kidnap President Kennedy's daughter Caroline.

DON'T FENCE HIM IN

Vice President Lyndon B. Johnson informs the Secret Service that he does not wish to be followed around by agents while in Washington.

"IF YOU'RE WHITE, YOU'RE ALRIGHT, IF YOU'RE BLACK, GET BACK"

Attorney General Robert F. Kennedy resigns from Washington's Metropolitan Club because of its "all-white" policy following a challenge to Mr. Kennedy's membership from the club's president Nelson T. Hartson.

OY VEY OM-ING

Israeli Premier David Ben-Gurion is off to Burma for a 10-day Buddhist meditation retreat in the home of Burma's Prime Minister U Nu.

Dancing Red, Blue And Green Sails In The Sunset

Beat poet Allen Ginsberg sails off to India in search of a mystical experience.

You Can Take The Boy Out Of The Altar But You Can't Take The Altar Out Of The Boy

35-year old ex-altar boy Robert F. Kennedy comes to the aid of a newly ordained priest volunteering to assist him at the 8:00 a.m. mass at St. Francis Xavier Roman Catholic Church in Hyannis, Massachusetts due to the absence of any altar boys.

HE'D WALK A MILE FOR A CAMEL

Taking up Vice President Lyndon B. Johnson's offer to come visit him in America, Pakistani camel driver Bashir Ahmed arrives in the U.S.

HEAVY DUTY READING

America's poet Carl Sandburg visits the new Carl Sandburg School in San Bruno, California.

With presidential aide and former Harvard historian Arthur Schlesinger, Jr. presiding, Robert F. Kennedy forms a book club dubbed Hickory Hill University whose members include Peace Corps Director Sargent Shriver, Deputy Defense Secretary Roswell Gilpatrick and Bobby's wife, Ethel.

10 MOST ADMIRED MEN

- President John F. Kennedy
- Former President Dwight D. Eisenhower
- Sir Winston Churchill
- Adlai E. Stevenson
- Dr. Albert Schweitzer
- Former President Harry S. Truman
- The Rev. Billy Graham
- Former Vice President Richard M. Nixon
- Pope John XXIII
- Former General of the Army Douglas MacArthur

10 MOST ADMIRED WOMEN

- Mrs. Eleanor Roosevelt
- Mrs. Jacqueline Kennedy
- Queen Elizabeth II
- Mrs. Dwight D. Eisenhower
- Mrs. Clare Boothe Luce
- Helen Keller
- Madame Chiang Kai-shek
- Senator Margaret Chase Smith
- Pauline Frederick
- Mrs. Patricia Nixon

In The Name Of LOVE

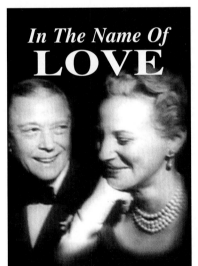

The Duke and Duchess of Windsor celebrate their 24th wedding anniversary. 25 years ago on December 11, 1936, Britain's King Edward VIII abdicated the throne to be with the woman he loved – Wallis Simpson.

The Anne Frank House opens in Amsterdam as an international youth center.

The George S. Patton, Jr. Memorial is dedicated at Saint-Symphorien, France honoring the World War II general who commanded the U.S. Third Army in Europe.

TIME MAN OF THE YEAR

John F. Kennedy

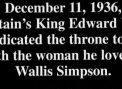

WHAT A YEAR IT WAS!

47

Exclusive from Parker

New Kind Of Pen You Can Fill 2 Ways!

takes America's largest ink cartridge

drinks ink from the bottle, too

PARKER 45

It's almost incredible. The new Parker 45 costs just $5, yet gives you features no other pen has—at any price. 1) It's a cartridge pen, easiest and cleanest fountain pen to fill. 2) It uses Super Quink in America's largest ink cartridge. Most economical, too—only 29¢ a five-pack. 3) You can also fill it from an ink bottle with its simple 95¢ converter. 4) You can change back and forth from cartridge-fill to bottle-fill whenever you want. 5) The point is 14 kt. gold; your choice of seven sizes from accountant style to very bold. This pen obeys—writes as only a superb Parker writing instrument can. Try it, the so-sensible Parker 45.

Memorable gift for grads, dads, birthdays and anniversaries.

$5

Other Parker 45's at $7.95, $8.75, $10.00. And at least look at the incomparable Parker 61, from $15.00 to $150.00.

ϕ THE PARKER PEN COMPANY — *Maker of the World's Most Wanted Pens*

Boxing For TOTS

It's time again for the Navy junior boxing finals at Annapolis. The 42nd in the series of bouts for pee-wee pugilists ranging from five to 14 years old and all raring to go.

Mike Webb, famous Navy boxing coach, presides and the first competitors have at it.

This is really the paper-weight division but these tiny tots with great big gloves learning to dish it out and to take it at an early age is Navy tradition.

The proud parents look on.

1961

THOSE BELLS ARE RINGING AGAIN

The Chicago ice cream 8-day strike involving 300 ice cream truck drivers and 700 inside employees is settled after, but not in time for, the Memorial Day weekend and the first heat wave of the summer.

The first U.S. disco called Le Club opens in Manhattan.

France introduces germ-free bank notes which prior to issuance are treated with a disinfectant.

CAMP FIRE GIRLS
mark their golden jubilee.

New nightsticks measuring two to four inches longer than the nightsticks being used by New York's finest since 1926 are introduced by Police Commissioner Stephen P. Kennedy.

Despite 20% fewer U.S. cows since 1950, their average annual milk output has increased by one-third per cow.

THAT'S A LOT OF CANS TO OPEN

One family in two owns a pet spending $3 billion a year to feed 90 million household animals.

Is Nothing Holy Anymore?

The U.S. seizes 2,700 pounds of Swiss cheese because artificial holes have been made with a mechanical device.

At the peak of rush hour on the hottest day in two years, a power blackout hits New York crippling a 5-square mile radius of Midtown Manhattan. Elevators halt, subways stall and air conditioners stop whirring, affecting the over 800,000 people who live or work in that area.

WHAT DID YOU SAY YOU WERE DOING DURING THE BLACKOUT?

Nine months after New York's four-hour blackout, the birth rate jumps.

• The postwar baby boom peaks with a record 4,282,000 births.

• Experiencing a "population explosion" now at 185 million, the U.S. ranks as the fourth largest nation following Communist China, India and the Soviet Union.

• Almost half of the 14-17-year old student population in the U.S. has worked this year.

• The U.S. Supreme Court refuses to overturn Connecticut's 19th Century law prohibiting the use of contraceptives.

• To help in family planning, the National Council of Churches approves the use of artificial methods of birth control.

WHAT A YEAR IT WAS!

Aviation News

There are no commercial aviation fatalities in the United States during the first six months of the year.

→ Air Force **Major Robert M. White** flies the X-15 experimental rocket plane at a speed of 3,603 mph.

→ In a test flight between Santa Catalina Island and San Diego, California a Convair 990 jetliner sets a world speed record for a commercial passenger transport flying 675 mph.

→ Averaging 576.72 mph, an American Airlines Boeing 707B sets a 4 hour, 29 minute commercial speed record flying from San Francisco to New York.

→ A New York-Paris nonstop flight is made in a record 3 hours, 19 minutes, 41 seconds by a U.S. jet bomber.

→ A tragic ending for Navy **Lieutenant Commander Victor G. Prather** when he dies of injuries suffered in a fall from a rescue helicopter. Earlier in the year he and another pilot set an altitude record of 21 1/2 miles in a 40-story high balloon.

→ **President Kennedy** orders modernization of the U.S. system of safe air traffic control and appoints a task force called "Project Beacon" to draft the program.

20 airlines begin using Los Angeles International Airport scheduled for completion in early 1962.

Vice President Lyndon B. Johnson speaks at the June 25th dedication of the Los Angeles International Airport.

Commander Alan B. Shepard, Jr. sets the record for the greatest altitude without earth orbit and the greatest mass lifted without earth orbit.

She'll Do Anything To Get Out Of The Kitchen

Setting a women's world endurance record, **Mrs. Alfred Wolfe** (56) stays up in the air in a 65-foot balloon for 40 hours, 8 minutes.

• **A**viatrix **Jacqueline Cochran** sets a new world speed record for women flying 842.6 mph in a Northrop T-38 Talon supersonic jet trainer.

• **F**lying without a co-pilot **Frances S. Bera** of Long Beach, California wins the Powder Puff Derby flying 2,709 miles in a Beechcraft E35 Bonanza.

THE BATTLE OF THE SEXES

Dating, Love, Marriage & The Whole Darn Thing

FAMOUS MEN

Reveal What They Find Particularly Unappealing About Women

Women Who:

- Come on too strong.
- Are unfeminine, messy or overweight.
- Wear curlers in public.
- Are late.
- Smoke excessively especially while eating.
- Give a fake kiss to avoid smearing their lipstick.
- Wear heavy make-up.
- Don't wear enough make-up.
- Wear pointed-toe shoes.
- Cry to win an argument.

ATTENTION ALL MEN

- Between the ages of 30 and 55 there are nearly 5,000,000 women without husbands, comprised of 2,000,000 single women with the balance being widows and divorcees.

- The divorce rate is two to three times higher in mixed religious marriages than in same faith marriages.

- Up to one couple in ten keeps their marriage a secret for a while.

HE'S A GOOD POTENTIAL HUSBAND IF HE'S:

1. Affectionate, loving and devoted.
2. Faithful and trustworthy.
3. Able to earn a decent living.
4. Honest and truthful with you.
5. Careful but not stingy with money.
6. Thoughtful and considerate of your wishes.
7. Pleasant and kind to your family.
8. Willing to confide in you.
9. Eager to work hard to get ahead.
10. Able to get along well with others.
11. A companion and partner.
12. Courteous and kind to you in public.
13. Willing to compromise when you disagree.
14. Fond of children.

SHE'S A GOOD POTENTIAL WIFE IF SHE'S:

1. Active and in good physical health.
2. Modest but not prudish.
3. Of appropriate height and weight.
4. Friendly and outgoing with people.
5. Attentive to her personal appearance.
6. Easy to talk to and confide in.
7. A good cook and housekeeper.
8. Has a nice sense of humor.
9. Helpful to others.
10. Respects and looks up to her husband.
11. Dances, plays cards and has good social skills.

MISS WORLD
Rosemarie Frankland
(Great Britain)

MISS AMERICA
Nancy Anne Fleming

MISS UNIVERSE
Marlene Schmidt
(West Germany)

EXCUSE ME, I THINK THAT PINK BUNK'S FOR ME

According to the commander of the armed forces police in Washington, D.C., Army service records indicate that at least one out of every 100 servicemen is homosexual and the figure could be as high as one in every 25.

BIGOTS AGAINST BAGELS

In violation of its national charter, the Alpha Tau Omega chapter at California's Stanford University pledges four Jewish students and faces disbarment.

THE TAX MAN COMETH

Rushing to marry before the April 6th deadline and thus raise the groom's personal income tax exemption from $392 to $692, 1,000 couples jam into Britain's Channel Island of Jersey for a honeymoon.

A HEADY EXPERIENCE

In what is called the greatest achievement in American mountaineering history, an Italian team scales the unclimbed south wall of Alaska's Mount McKinley in a month-long climb.

HEY BUDDY CAN YOU SPARE THE TIME?

*Oregon's **Governor Mark O. Hatfield** signs law approving daylight saving-time in the Portland metropolitan area with the rest of the state remaining on standard time.*

In Chicago an experiment to employ mentally retarded people gets underway in a nonprofit pet and garden shop where they care for animals and organize garden supplies.

MORE TO COME

As a preview of **Macy's 4th of July celebration,** over one million people turn out to see the department store's fireworks display over the Hudson.

TAI-CHI CHUAN is introduced into the United States by U.N. employee **Da Liu**, who has been practicing this system of exercises for more than 28 years and is considered a master.

PIER PRESSURE

Quaint beach resort SANTA MONICA rated no. 1 vacation spot by the Official Vacation Guide to Southern California.

L.A. IS BURNING

In what is called the worst fire in the city's history 3,500 people flee their homes in the Santa Monica Mountains as over 400 homes are destroyed including the homes of **Burt Lancaster, Joe E. Brown, Walter Wanger** and **Zsa Zsa Gabor.**

WHAT A YEAR IT WAS!

61

1961

Forty additional scrolls are found in the Dead Sea caves in Israel.

The oldest known home of primitive man in the Southeast U.S. is established near Bridgeport, Alabama as Russell Cave National Monument.

The remains of a palace thought to be the home of Augustus, the first Roman emperor who lived 27 B.C. through 14 A.D., is discovered in Rome.

EXCUSE ME, WHERE'S THE TREADMILL?

A training gym used by gladiators of Domitian's reign from 81-96 A.D. is excavated in Rome.

Them Bones, Them Bones, Them Thigh Bones

In Tripoli, Libya, American and French oilmen discover a graveyard of prehistoric beasts while drilling in the desert of southwest Cyrenaica.

EXTRA

ALL THE NEWS FIT TO PRINT ALL THE TIME

THE NEW YORK TIMES is the country's best newspaper according to a poll of 276 dailies.

THE NEW YORK TIMES begins preparations for a West Coast edition to begin next year.

GOOD GRIEF, WHO'S THIS FRIEDA?

Curly haired Frieda is the latest character to join the PEANUTS gang read daily by more than 38 million fans.

HAPPY BIRTHDAY DICK

DICK TRACY celebrates his 30th birthday as a major comic strip.

WE'RE NOT JOKING AROUND ABOUT THIS

Comic book production rises with about 30,000,000 copies published each month.

In an attempt to find a new, young audience, **The Saturday Evening Post** tries a modern look.

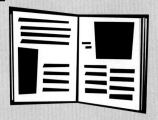

Reader's Digest holds the lead in circulation while the **Ladies' Home Journal** loses its #1 position in women's magazines to **McCall's**.

WHAT A YEAR IT WAS!

New Words & Expressions

ANTI-METRO
Those against bureaucratic interference in city planning.

AUTOINSTRUCTIONAL
Teaching one's self using available materials.

BIRCHER
A person belonging to the John Birch Society.

COMSYMP
An expression coined by the John Birch Society to describe supposed Communist sympathizers.

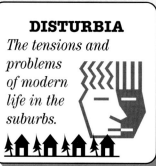

DISTURBIA
The tensions and problems of modern life in the suburbs.

EARTHSHAKE
When the ground moves due to natural or other reasons such as an atomic explosion.

FREEDOM RIDER
Those who ride desegregated buses in areas where segregation is rampant to try to eliminate racial discrimination.

EXOSOCIETY
The existence of intelligent life forms beyond our galaxy.

MOON-CRAWLER
A remote-controlled automobile built to drive on the moon.

MICROELECTRONICS
The branch of science that creates diminutive electronic parts.

MUSCLE SHIRT
A T-Shirt without sleeves that shows off the wearer's muscles.

NUCLEAR EXCURSION
An uncontainable nuclear reaction.

PARAGNOST
A person with psychic powers.

READ-IN
Blacks who defy custom and/or law and demonstrate at white libraries. Similar to sit-in.

SELF-CONTAINED CLASSROOM
When one instructor is in charge of a classroom.

SKYJACKER
One who hijacks a plane in transit.

SPACEPHOBIA
Dread of the universe's outer regions.

TROIKA
A regime consisting of three people. A Russian term.

WHODUNITRY
Private eye tales.

UNISPHERE
An enormous globe created as the emblem for the 1964 New York World's Fair.

WEBSTER'S THIRD NEW INTERNATIONAL DICTIONARY *is published with almost 1/2 million entries.*

THIS IS NO SHAGGY DOG TAIL

According to the American Kennel Club, poodles remain in first place for the total number of registrations.

CONGRATULATIONS, MOM

Strelka, one of the animals that made the first space ride in 1960, gives birth to a litter of puppies.

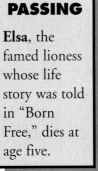

PASSING

Elsa, the famed lioness whose life story was told in "Born Free," dies at age five.

GO BANG YOUR HEAD AGAINST A BEAM

According to a zoologist at London's Queen Mary College, termites warn each other about approaching enemy ants by banging their heads on the beams they are currently snacking on.

A handler is crushed to death in Florida by a 2,342-pound, 22-foot long python.

An article in *PTA Magazine* on the dating habits of American youngsters reveals that dating begins as early as nine years old with some 12-year olds already going steady.

Teenagers rank a kind heart and consideration for others as the basis of good manners and the key to popularity.

Water Roaches	=	Lifeguards
Zen	=	Wild or unusual
Peter Gunn	=	A sophisticate
Unborn	=	Naïve
Sled	=	Non-hot-rod car
Nurd	=	A peculiar person
Pale One	=	Intellectual
Zoros	=	Jitters
Monster	=	The Telephone

A Good Relationship With Your Parents Should Include The Following:

- *You confide in them.*
- *You treat them with respect.*
- *You want to please them.*
- *You discuss your friends with them.*
- *You bring friends home.*
- *You show an interest in what's going on at home.*
- *You do your chores.*
- *You follow the family rules.*
- *You behave sensibly and reliably.*
- *You discuss future plans.*

BUSINESS 1961

FUTURE JOBS

Here's what youngsters entering the workplace in the next decade can expect:

- Jobs Requiring More Education
- Expanded Technical Positions
- Less Farm Work
- More Competition
- Shorter Work Week With Increased Salary
- More Women In The Work Force
- Automation Will Replace Some Jobs

THE JOB INTERVIEW
To Hire Or Not To Hire

WAYS TO LOSE:
- Poor Conduct
- Smugness
- Sloppy Grooming
- Aggressive Behavior

WAYS TO WIN:
- Act Enthusiastic
- Speak Well
- Neatness
- Listen
- Come Prepared

Lockheed Aircraft
President Courtland Gross signs a pact pledging fairness for all workers regardless of race. V.P. Lyndon B. Johnson, Chairman of the President's Equal Employment Opportunity Committee, also signs.

Manufacturers Trust Company and **Hanover Bank** merge, becoming the 4th biggest bank in the country, **Manufacturers Hanover Trust Company**.

AUTO NEWS

German automaker Volkswagen makes over one million vehicles and is the world's 56th biggest company.

The 5th annual International Auto Show opens in New York, displaying 400 cars from ten nations.

Ford Motors buys Philco.

In a new agreement, American Motors agrees to employee profit sharing.

WESTINGHOUSE CELEBRATES ITS 75TH ANNIVERSARY.

Here are the number of hours it takes the average factory employee to buy:

PRODUCT	HOURS
Car	975
Vacuum Cleaner	26
Refrigerator	71
Men's Suit	17
Dress	1 3/4

Following the success of the PLAYBOY CLUB in Chicago, a second club opens in Miami.

PLAYBOY'S HUGH HEFNER begins publishing the magazine "Show Business Illustrated."

IBM CHAIRMAN OF THE BOARD THOMAS J. WATSON, JR. EXTENDS INTEREST-FREE LOANS TO EMPLOYEES WHO WANT TO BUILD BOMB SHELTERS.

The minimum wage is raised from $1.00 to $1.15.

The average amount of money required weekly by American families to survive is $84.

The typical wage increase for approximately three million American workers is **8.2 cents an hour**.

1961

UNION NEWS

The International Brotherhood of Teamsters is barred reentry into the AFL-CIO.

The International Brotherhood of Teamsters reelects **James R. Hoffa** president. His salary is increased from $50,000 to $75,000.

John L. Lewis comes out of retirement to defend a $40 million loan given to the West Kentucky Coal Co. by the United Mine Workers.

Lewis

I'M A LITTLE TEAPOT, SHORT AND STOUT

Production is halted at a British Ford Motor plant when management complains about the employees' tea breaks and preference for brewing their own tea. The 400 workers refuse to drink the weak company-brewed tea and the company backs down after two days.

Throughout the year approximately 3,300 strikes involving almost 1-1/2 million workers effects U.S. businesses, the fewest strikes since the close of World War II. The longest strikes include Philadelphia's Operating Engineers for 61 days and Sheet Metal Workers in Minneapolis-St. Paul for 58 days.

A wildcat strike by flight engineers lasts six days and effects seven major airlines, including TWA, American and Eastern, virtually halting air travel and costing the industry $40 million. A President Kennedy-appointed commission analyzes the situation and succeeds in ending the strike.

President Kennedy invokes the Taft-Hartley Act to end a maritime strike by approximately 80,000 members of five different unions on the West, East and Gulf coasts.

The United Auto Workers shut down 92 out of 129 General Motors plants for two weeks.

One hundred thousand commuters in the New York area must find different ways of getting to work when New York tugboat and ferry crews strike for two weeks. Some railroad workers refuse to cross the picket lines, effecting even more commuters. Governor Nelson Rockefeller and Secretary of Labor Arthur J. Goldberg get involved and help resolve the situation by meeting with strike leaders.

I WAS WORKING ON THE RAILROAD

Railroad work continues to decline, reaching a century low of 717,000 people.

The Order of Railroad Telegraphers comes to an agreement with Southern Pacific guaranteeing the telegraphers work for life.

Twenty-nine electrical firms including General Electric and Westinghouse are convicted of price-fixing and unfair bidding practices. Individual executives are also found guilty. Attorney General Robert Kennedy considers the offenses "so willful and flagrant that even more severe sentences would have been appropriate."

WHAT A YEAR IT WAS!

sTOCKs 1961

SOYBEANS ARE THE #1 COMMODITY TRADED AT THE CHICAGO BOARD OF TRADE.

For the first time in over twenty years, the SEC investigates the **AMERICAN STOCK EXCHANGE.**

THE DOW-JONES INDUSTRIAL INDEX REACHES A RECORD-HIGH OF 734.91.

Alcoa	75
Bulova	19
Chrysler	44
Coca Cola	93 $1/8$
Conde Nast	14 $3/8$
Disney	41
Firestone	42
Heinz	58
Hershey's	150 $1/2$
Hewlett Packard	40 $5/8$
IBM	579
MCA	81
Motorola	97 $1/2$
Texaco	54 $7/8$
Xerox	166

ROUGHLY ONE BILLION SHARES ARE TRADED ON THE NEW YORK STOCK EXCHANGE.

AN INTERNATIONAL STOCK EXCHANGE IS CREATED, THE FEDERATION INTERNATIONALE DE BOURSES DE VALEURS, AND INCLUDES PARIS, LONDON, MADRID, AMSTERDAM AND MILAN.

Fast food maker Ray Kroc buys out the **MCDONALD** brothers for $2.7 million.

Hey Kids, The Iced Tea Man Is Coming.
Good Humor is bought by Lipton.

SONY CORPORATION of Japan sells common stock in America for the first time.

TIFFANY & CO. is sold by **GENESCO, INC.** to investors headed by Tiffany Chairman Walter Hoving.

The Justice Department assembles a grand jury to probe into business practices of the entertainment industry, especially those of MCA.

Yes, Virginia, There Is A Santa Claus For $3.99

Montgomery Ward's Christmas catalogue causes a furor by having a picture of "dad" trimming the tree instead of Santa. Chairman John A. Barr responds to each parent's complaint letter personally, sending along Christmas books for the youngsters.

THE YO-YO CRAZE *hits coast to coast, and to keep up with the increased demand 1,200 Duncan Yo-Yo's are made per hour, 24 hours a day.*

The Empire State Building is sold for $65 million, the most ever spent on one building.

WAGES

WEEKLY

Coal Miner	$ 128
Construction Worker	127
Factory Worker	96
Proofreader	85
Receptionist	75
Retail Sales	72

YEARLY

President John F. Kennedy	$ 100,000
Chief Justice Earl Warren	35,500
Vice President Lyndon B. Johnson	35,000
Top Executive, Japan	30,000
Physicist	20,000
Pharmacist	7,000
Railroad Worker	6,400
Assistant D.A. Suffolk County, Massachusetts	5,000-8,000
Farm Hand	1,900

THE NUMBERS

Consumer Price Index, avg.	127.8
Gross National Product	$520 billion
Unemployment, avg.	5 million
Workers	68 $1/2$ million (all-time high)

A fixed-term certificate of deposit is now available at the First National City Bank of New York.

1961

This Is THE PRICE THAT WAS

UNDER $ 1.00

Address Labels (500)	$ .25
Aluminum Foil	.49
Band Aids	.69
Broom	.98
Car Wash	.75
Mouthwash	.49
Paper Towels	.31

UNDER $ 1.00

Pillow Case	$ .99
Soap	.05
Stud Finder	.50
Tissues	.29
Toothpaste	.53
Washcloth	.39

FOOD

Angel Food Cake	
Apple Sauce (16 oz.)	$ .59
Apples (lb.)	.10
Artichokes (each)	.10
Avocados (each)	.10
Bananas (lb.)	.19
Bell Peppers (lb.)	.10
Bread (loaf)	.15
Butter (lb.)	.19
Cake Mix	.69
Cantaloupe (lb.)	.29
Celery (lb.)	.05
Cheddar Cheese (lb.)	.07
Coffee (lb.)	.65
Cola	.49
Corn on the Cob (each)	.10
	.05

FOOD

Cottage Cheese (pint)	$ .25
Crackers (lb.)	.27
Cucumbers (each)	.05
Eggs (dz.)	.45
Grapes (lb.)	.19
Ice Cream (1/2 gallon)	.69
Lemons (lb.)	.10
Lettuce (head)	.10
Mayonnaise (qt.)	.39
Nectarines (lb.)	.10
Oranges (lb.)	.10
Peaches (lb.)	.10
Peanut Butter (lb.)	.39
Peas (lb.)	.10
Pineapple (lb.)	.10
Pound Cake	.49

WHAT A YEAR IT WAS!

L'HOMME

Basketball	$ 8.45
Briefs	1.25
Electric Shaver	24.95
Golf Cart	39.95
Slacks	17.75-24.50
Sport Shirt	7.95
Stetson Hat	15.95
Suit	55.00-135.00
Swim Trunks	5.95
T-Shirt	1.50

La FEMME

Bra	$ 3.95
Crepe Dress	19.95
Evan Picone Suit: Jacket	35.00
Skirt	30.00
Irish Linen Jacket	14.95
Lipstick	2.00
Nail Polish	.95
Nylons	1.15-1.65
Shoes	8.95-14.95
Sunglasses	1.98

FOR THE HOME

Clock Radio	$ 24.95
Diapers (dz.)	1.98
Dryer	168.77
Electric Blanket	28.00
Fallout Shelter	150.00
Folding Chair	9.95
Hamper	8.95
Ironing Board	8.88
LP's	4.98
Paint (gallon)	6.69
Percolator (12 cup)	22.86
Pressure Cooker	12.95
Refrigerator	199.95
Scale	3.99
Screwdriver	2.00
Shower Curtain	4.00

FOR THE HOME

Steam Iron	$ 15.99
Stepladder	2.99
Sterling Silver Candlesticks	8.98
Television (19")	199.95
Washing Machine	248.77
Water Heater (20 gallon)	43.97
Wrench	1.75

HOUSING

3 bedroom house in:

Venice, CA	$ 15,500
Topanga Canyon, CA	17,000
Princeton, New Jersey	19,500
Marina del Rey, CA	21,500
Teaneck, New Jersey	26,000
Stamford, CT	28,500

THE HIGH COST OF WAR

Arms, yearly (America)	$ 46 billion
Arms, hourly (world)	14 million
Arms, yearly, per person (world)	40.00

Americans spend approximately $2 billion on toys this year.

MACY's

in Manhattan presents the classic Benny Goodman Quartet for a day to entertain shoppers and promote purchasing. Band members include Gene Krupa, Lionel Hampton and Teddy Wilson.

The U.S. Supreme Court rules against E.I. du Pont de Nemours & Co. and forces the company to rid itself of 63 million shares of General Motors stock within ten years.

Interest on U.S. Government
E and H bonds
increases to 3 3/4 percent.

Continental Airlines announces plans to create an additional class of airline service, less expensive than coach and first class.

TWA files a civil antitrust suit against founder Howard Hughes.

 PASSINGS

JAMES FORD BELL, founder and former chairman of the board of General Mills, Inc., dies at age 81, only weeks after his wife passes on.

Founder of Yellow Cab Co. and the Hertz method of renting cars, JOHN D. HERTZ dies at age 82.

1961 ADVERTISEMENT

 ...sensation of the year!

by

OLDS

Everyone's talking about the new Starfire . . . because there's nothing else like it! Oldsmobile's spectacular new full-size sports convertible is custom-crafted with contoured bucket seats and center control console. And it's powered for the adventurous . . . with ultra-high compression, multijet carburetion, high performance camshaft and high-torque rear axle! See what all the excitement's about . . . at your Olds Quality Dealer's!

OLDSMOBILE DIVISION • GENERAL MOTORS CORPORATION

Twin top-grain leather bucket seats and sports-type control console add distinction to the sensational Starfire!

SCIENCE 1961
MAN CONQUERS SPACE

Man has his first great success in space as Russian cosmonaut Yuri Gagarin becomes the first man to orbit the earth.

Accompanied by Nikita Khrushchev (above) Gagarin receives a hero's welcome from the excited crowd who strain to get a look at their hero. It is the propaganda coup of the year.

U.S. DETERMINED TO CATCH

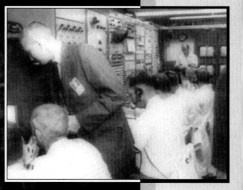

Following the success of the Russian flight, U.S. space plans are immediately accelerated. President Kennedy commits to having a man on the moon by the end of the decade.

With the whole world watching, the **Mercury** capsule is right on course on its suborbital flight as Commander Alan B. Shepard, Jr. takes over the controls, becoming the first man to guide a spacecraft.

UP IN THE SPACE WAR

115 miles up, he went 300 miles downrange right on target and is picked up by waiting helicopters.

The triumph of Alan B. Shepard, Jr., U.S. space pioneer.

Following in Commander Shepard's star-studded footsteps is Captain Virgil I. "Gus" Grissom who rides a **Mercury** capsule to an altitude of 118 miles in a 16-minute flight, making him the second American and third human to be in space.

The crew on the rescue carrier watches and everything is A-OK until the heart-breaking finale. As the Captain prepared to leave the capsule, explosive bolts on the escape hatch let go and the **Mercury** is lost.

Despite the partial failure of the mission, man is getting closer to the moon.

1961

BRITISH PHYSICIST SIR JOHN COCKCROFT RECEIVES THE 1961 ATOMS FOR PEACE AWARD.

CO-WINNER OF THE NOBEL PRIZE IN CHEMISTRY 10 YEARS AGO FOR THE DISCOVERY OF PLUTONIUM, GLENN THEODORE SEABORG IS APPOINTED CHAIRMAN OF THE ATOMIC ENERGY COMMISSION.

Nobel Prizes

PHYSIOLOGY or MEDICINE
George von Bekesy, USA

CHEMISTRY
Melvin Calvin, USA

PHYSICS
Robert Hofstadter, USA
Rudolf L. Mossbauer, Germany

ATOMS ON ICE

The Atomic Energy Commission ships the first nuclear power plant to Antarctica.

In an unexplained explosion, three men die in the first fatal nuclear reactor accident at an Atomic Energy Commission station in Idaho.

The first giant generator of the Robert Moses Niagara Power Plant begins delivering power in February.

BOMBS

✹ At the Reggane testing grounds in the Sahara, France executes its fourth atomic test.

✹ Ending a three-year moratorium, Russia detonates an atomic bomb over Siberia. Six weeks later, ruthlessly disregarding an appeal from the United Nations to halt the massive blast, the Soviets discharge a 50 megaton bomb, making it the biggest explosion ever made by man.

✹ The U.S. resumes atomic testing setting off a small underground explosion in Nevada.

✹ The biggest man-made nonnuclear surface explosion in history takes place in Alberta, Canada with a 100-ton blast of TNT.

• The Soviets brag that they have solved the problem of "destroying missiles in flight" after they detonate a 30-megaton nuclear bomb.

• According to the U.S. Army its **Nike-Zeus** antimissile missile has successfully intercepted a missile in flight for the first time.

• **Plasma**, the fourth state of matter, has been successfully stabilized by Swedish physicists, a vital step in harnessing of the H-Bomb for peaceful purposes.

• Carlsbad, New Mexico is the detonation site of a nuclear device in the first atoms for peace test.

• The Strategic Air Command launches the first solid-fuel rocket, the **Minuteman**, an intercontinental ballistic missile (ICBM) which is successfully fired from Cape Canaveral, Florida traveling a distance of 4,200 miles.

WHAT A YEAR IT WAS!

The world's longest promontory, the Antarctic promontory, also called the **Antarctic Peninsula,** *is found to be 1,200 miles long, 200 miles longer than previous calculations.*

American geologist **Harry Hess** *of Princeton University develops a revolutionary new theory of continental drift proposing that continents move because they float on huge plates of heavier rock that make up the earth's crust.*

The discovery of the element **lawrencium,** no. 103 on the periodic scale, is announced by the U.S. Atomic Energy Commission.

EUREKA WE'VE FOUND OMEGA!

Omega meson, a new particle of matter, is discovered by scientists at the Lawrence Radiation Laboratory of the University of California.

"Brave New World" Revisited

Aldous, a computer with a personality and emotional reactions such as love, fear and anger, is created by Dr. John C. Loehlin of the University of Nebraska.

UNDER A BLANKET OF PURPLE

U.S. Air Force scientists discover a three-mile layer of "haze" in the upper atmosphere which might be responsible for producing the "purple light" seen during twilight.

• Two rooms believed to be part of the great Roman emperor Augustus' home are found in Rome with the painted frescoes still vibrant in color after 2,000 years.

• Dating back 8,000 years, 1,000 mud-brick houses containing frescoes, statuettes, hunting equipment and household utensils are discovered in Turkey.

• A ship that sank during the Trojan War is discovered off the coast of Turkey.

• Water taken from deep desert wells in Saudi Arabia appears to date back 20,000-25,000 years.

Radioactive dating places primitive toolmaking man on earth 1,750,000 years ago.

SOMETHING TO GRUNT ABOUT

British scientist S.B. Leakey discovers bones of the oldest human ever found while digging in Tanganyika. The specimen, estimated to be the remains of an 11-year old Australopithecus, appears to have died by violent means.

WHAT A YEAR IT WAS!

75

1961

SOVIETS LAUNCH HEAVIEST SATELLITE – SPUTNIK V, WEIGHING 7.1 TONS.

An **Atlas** rocket is destroyed along with its monkey "passenger" when it veers off course after launch from Cape Canaveral, Florida.

Ham, a 37 1/2 lb. trained chimpanzee, is the first chimp in space, making an 18-minute suborbital flight as a prelude to Alan B. Shepard, Jr.'s mission.

NO MONKEYING AROUND HERE

A male chimp named **Enos** is picked up from the Atlantic recovery zone 250 miles south of Bermuda after he successfully completes two revolutions of the earth after being projected into orbit in a U.S. Project **Mercury** space capsule.

THIS IS A REAL RAT

French rocket **Veronique**, with a rat on-board, is recovered after going up 95 miles.

AFTER ORBITING THE EARTH 17 TIMES IN 25 HOURS, 18 MINUTES, SOVIET COSMONAUT MAJOR GHERMAN S. TITOV LANDS SAFELY.

• U.S. tests *Ranger I*, an instrument satellite designed for a 1962 moon landing, putting it into orbit at Cape Canaveral.

• A "dummy astronaut" is recovered after circling the earth once in a 2,700-lb. U.S. Project *Mercury* capsule sent into orbit from Cape Canaveral.

IT ISN'T RAINING RAIN YOU KNOW, IT'S RAINING COSMIC RAYS

The biggest cosmic ray shower to be recorded supports the theory that high-energy cosmic ray particles originate outside our galaxy.

• Satellite *Explorer XI* launched by NASA carrying telescope to hunt gamma rays.

• Houston, Texas is selected as the site for the new $60,000,000 manned spacecraft center which will serve as command center for NASA's Project *Apollo*, a program aimed at placing men on the moon by 1970.

• Venus rotates just once in 250 days according to American astronomers Roland L. Carpenter and Richard M. Goldstein and unlike other planets in the solar system turns from east to west.

Little Joe 5B proves MERCURY escape system infallible in final test flight.

New record altitude for a helicopter is 32,000 feet set by Air Force craft at Bloomfield, Connecticut.

Russia announces that it has successfully flown a nuclear-powered bomber for 21 days without refueling.

• Based on the discovery of new star clusters that are 20 to 30 billion years old, it is now believed that the universe could be at least twice as old as previously thought.

• Astronomer Carl Sagan of the University of California theorizes that the possibility of life on Jupiter is somewhat better than the possibility of life on Venus.

25-year old Maynard "Red" Berg becomes the first paraplegic in history to stand through the activity of his own muscles due to a new technique called "bioelectronics" which uses an electrical device hooked up to the patient that transmits messages to the muscles.

Electronic devices will eventually bring light to the blind and hearing to the deaf according to noted Israeli physicist and electronics engineer Professor Franz Ollendorff of the Israel Institute of Technology.

WHAT A YEAR IT WAS!

The First Hydrofoil Ship–The **H.S. Denison**– Is Designed.

The U.S. nuclear submarine **U.S.S. Patrick Henry**, loaded with 16 Polaris missiles, sets an underwater cruising record of 66 days, 22 hours on its arrival at its base at Holy Lock, Scotland from Charleston, South Carolina.

The world's fastest nuclear submarine, the **U.S.S. Thresher**, joins fleet at Portsmouth, New Hampshire.

The world's fastest submarine – **U.S.S. Shark** – joins the U.S. Navy fleet at Newport News, Virginia.

Bethlehem Steel unveils the first nuclear-powered surface warship, **U.S.S. Long Beach**, in Quincy, Massachusetts.

Vice-Admiral Hyman G. Rickover tells a joint atomic energy subcommittee that a drawing accompanying a toy model of the **Polaris** submarine that sells for $2.98 has given the Soviet Union millions of dollars worth of information about U.S. nuclear submarines.

Two new supercarriers are commissioned by the U.S. Navy – the **Kitty Hawk** and the **Constellation**.

The world's largest ship, nuclear-powered submarine **U.S.S. Enterprise** capable of carrying seven aircraft squadrons, completes sea trials in November.

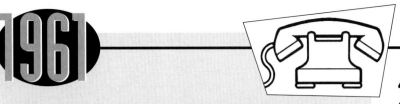

1961

President Kennedy gives an official go-ahead to the electronics industry to establish privately-owned space satellite communications systems.

Hello, This Is Your Queenie

A telephone conversation between Queen Elizabeth II and Canadian Prime Minister Diefenbaker inaugurates the new trans-atlantic submarine telephone cable between Great Britain and Canada, the first link in a proposed around-the-world Commonwealth system.

A new coast-to-coast transcontinental microwave system scheduled for completion next year gets under way.

45 U.S. cities now have telex services.

- - - - -

A five-year project to index the plant world on 50,000 computer punch cards kicks off at the Connecticut Agricultural Experiment Station in New Haven.

- - - - -

An article appearing in "Data Processing" magazine reports that 4,927 commercial digital computers, including 51 different models, are now in use.

- - - - -

The IBM computer **Stretch** is capable of translating Russian into English at 60,000 words an hour.

- - - - -

Linking a computer, tape-punching typewriter and a photographic typesetting machine, Massachusetts Institute of Technology develops a system that can produce a 400-page book in a few hours.

NASA selects RCA to build the first U.S. experimental communications satellite.

New weather satellite Tiros III makes history as it transmits early-warning pictures to earth of the cloud formations that develop into a hurricane.

The Jet Propulsion Laboratory of the California Institute of Technology makes direct radar contact with the planet Venus.

BREAKING THE GENETIC CODE

For the first time, DNA, the essence of heredity, is extracted virtually intact from human sperm by Drs. Ellen Borenfreund and Aaron Bendich.

A new amino acid has been found
in collagen making it the first time in 25 years
that an amino acid with a basically new
structure has been discovered.

Research into genetic code clues is being conducted at the
National Institute of Health headed by Drs. Marshall W. Nirenberg and
J. Heinrich Matthaei and at the NYU School of Medicine headed by
Dr. Severo Ochoa, who won a Nobel Prize for his work on RNA.

THE WART VIRUS IS ISOLATED AND 10 OF 20 PEOPLE ARE SUCCESSFULLY REINOCULATED.

Outbreaks of infectious hepatitis in Mississippi and Alabama are blamed on shellfish for the first time.

---

385 tons of grains, leafy vegetables and peanuts are seized due to excessive amounts of pesticides.

A flavoring agent, safrole, used in soft drinks and other foods, has been banned because it is found to be carcinogenic.

Physicians in Los Angeles, California advise 10,000 of their patients to move out of the Basin because of air pollution, which is thought to be a factor in lung diseases.

Air tested in about 100 cities throughout the U.S. reveals the presence of cancer-producing pollutants which, when tested in animals, caused cancer. These pollutants are 100 or more times the amounts found in rural areas.

Tests conducted at the University of Minnesota Medical School prove that it's safe to fluoridate water supplies according to Dr. W.D. Armstrong, physiological chemistry professor at the school.

WHAT A YEAR IT WAS!

Your Chevy dealer has a perfect match of value and variety

(That's why so many budget-wise young couples start off right—with an OK Used Car!)

In fact, that's why—young and old—thousands of bargain-lovin' folks buy at an OK lot. Low price tags and spunky used cars are an irresistible combination!

You get this combination because again this year more people are buying Chevrolets than any other make. So you'll find plenty of trade-ins—perky "young 'uns," solid-stepping "middle-agers," and some top-condition "senior citizens," too, for you folks who really want to save.

All your Chevy dealer's used cars and trucks are good buys. But the very best on his lot—the ones with plenty of *unused* miles left in them—are those he selects as OK Used Cars.

USED OK CARS
CHEVROLET

For the best Used Car buy go where you see the OK sign

SEE YOUR LOCAL AUTHORIZED CHEVROLET DEALER

Medicine 1961

Types I and II of the oral live-virus polio vaccine developed by Albert Sabin are licensed by the U.S. Public Health Service.

AMA
AMERICAN MEDICAL ASSOCIATION

American Medical Association delegates endorse the "live" Sabin polio vaccine over the Salk vaccine.

An article published in the AMA journal warns that the overuse of antibiotics is resulting in germs becoming resistant, allowing them to continue to survive and multiply.

The AMA reports a definite link between heart disease and smoking as a result of a study of 3,000 smoking and non-smoking men.

Basing its decision on available evidence, the AMA Council on Drugs does not believe the estrogen cancer scare is justified.

 **PASSING**

CARL JUNG, psychology pioneer who believed religion and race memory were strong factors in one's psyche, dies at age 85. Jung created the concepts of archetypes, inferiority complex and collective unconscious as well as the personality types introvert and extrovert.

A U.S. Senate subcommittee headed by Estes Kefauver reports that prescription drug prices are unreasonably high.

AVERAGE ANNUAL MEDICAL EXPENSES

Doctor Bills:	$26.00
Hospital Care:	31.00
Medicines & Glasses:	26.50
Dental Care:	10.50
Misc. Health Needs:	6.00
Total Per Person	**$100.00**

the "conspiracy of silence"

practiced by most doctors and relatives on dying patients is decried by two Boston physicians who believe the patient has the right to know.

1961

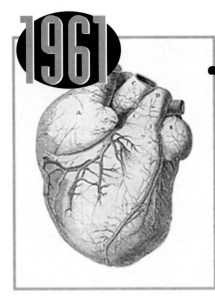

You gotta have heart.

Speaking at a conference, Dr. Irvine H. Page, director of research of the Cleveland Clinic Foundation, advises that keeping weight down and exercise such as bicycle riding are excellent ways to reduce heart attacks.

 A non-surgical external cardiac massage method for starting a heart that has stopped beating is demonstrated at Johns Hopkins Hospital which involves putting pressure on the patient's breastbone.

 For emergency treatment of heart attack victims, a new combination of mouth-to-mouth resuscitation and external cardiac massage is demonstrated at Johns Hopkins Hospital.

 Arteriosclerosis, commonly known as hardening of the arteries, is the chief problem in the field of heart disease from which 500,000 Americans die each year, amounting to twice the toll from cancer and five times the deaths from automobile accidents.

 University of Minnesota's physiologist **Ancel Keys**, author of last year's best-selling book "Eat Well and Stay Well," criticizes the eating habits of Americans saying that they eat too much food, especially foods containing saturated fat such as meat, milk, butter and ice cream, which leads to coronary disease.

 The American Heart Association, in the random testing of 100 children between the ages of three and seven, finds more than half have harmless heart murmurs which are likely to disappear during adolescence.

 The President's Conference on Heart Disease and Cancer reveals that at least two people die from heart disease and cancer every minute in the U.S.

DOCTOR, HEAL THYSELF

Of the 2,000 doctors taking medical examinations during an American Medical Association convention, an estimated one in five are found to be suffering from heart abnormalities.

SKIPPING A FEW BEATS HERE AND THERE

The British medical journal THE PRACTITIONER reports on a successful technique to reduce a heart patient's temperature safely to 15°C at which time the heart can be stopped for up to 55 minutes during an operation.

THE SMOKING LUNG

Latest statistics released by the American Cancer Society's Cancer Prevention Study reveal that the more deeply a smoker inhales the greater the death rate.

Two out of three doctors agree that cigarette smoking is a major cause of lung cancer.

WHAT A YEAR IT WAS!

Don't have one for the road

In experiments conducted at Yale under a grant from the U.S. Public Health Service, small amounts of alcohol appear to improve problem solving.

In a paper published in the "Michigan State Bar Journal," psychiatrist Melvin L. Selzer writes that the alcoholic rather than the casual drinker is the cause of many accidents with about 50% of car fatalities caused by excessive drinking.

The most popular illegal drug sold in America is amphetamines or "pep pills" used by truck drivers to stay awake on their long hauls.

LET THEM EAT DRUGS
The Joint Commission on Mental Illness and Health reports that of the 500,000 patients in 277 state mental hospitals, more than half receive no active treatment.

IF THEY DON'T LIKE IT, GIVE 'EM DRUGS
Dr. Irving A. Kraft, director of the child study clinic of the Houston State Psychiatric Institute, reports success in treating school-phobic children with tranquilizers with 62% of them returning to school within two weeks after being put on drugs.

FIVE MILLION AMERICANS are confirmed alcoholics with one out of every 15 people who drinks becoming an alcoholic.

DRINKING TO STAY SOBER

As a means of surviving our hectic lives Britain's **Dr. B.G. Lucas** recommends the use of alcohol and sedatives stating their use "is necessary for man's continued existence in our so-called civilized world."

A BREAKFAST OF CHAMPIONS

Experiments conducted in the workplace show that individuals who eat a good breakfast without a mid-morning coffee break produce more work than their non-breakfast eating counterparts who take that morning break.

Stanford University Medical Center in Palo Alto, California reports that the morning coffee break is essential as coffee drinkers need that caffeine fix to keep them alert, talkative and more motivated to work.

STORK COSTS FLYING HIGH

The cost of having a baby has increased from $193 to $272 – a 41% increase in five years.

AVERAGE LIFE EXPECTANCY

70

about 22 years longer than your grandparents.

A study at Baltimore City Hospital shows that excessive smoking by pregnant women increases the risk of premature birth.

PUTTING PUPPY ON THE PILL

A new oral contraceptive for dogs called Prodox has been developed by Upjohn Co. which delays the female's fertility cycle.

• U.S. physician Jack Lippes introduces a birth control method called the IUD.

New York doctor Robert W. Hillman concludes that the growth of fingernails and hair increases significantly during pregnancy.

An Italian research team experiments successfully with repeated fertilization of human eggs.

NASTY LITTLE BUGGER

The respiratory syncytial virus is identified as a major cause of severe respiratory illness in infants and the common cold in adults.

HOW TO KEEP A MAN

- Remain loving.

- Enjoy being kissed.

- Have a good sense of humor.

- Stay limber.

- Be a little crazy once in a while.

1961

DRILLING FOR DOLLARS

Americans rack up a total of over 700,000,000 cavities or about four per person.

THERE'S A WHOLE LOT OF GUMMIN' GOING ON

22,000,000 Americans don't have a tooth in their mouths.

DON'T BRUSH THIS OFF LIGHTLY

To prevent premature loss of the first set of molars, Dr. Roy M. Wolff tells the Greater New York Dental Meeting that parents should brush their children's teeth preferably until the child is 9 or 10. He also recommends that teeth be brushed immediately following a candy bar or soda pop to prevent tooth decay.

When having a tooth drilled or getting an injection, keep your eyes open as you feel more pain in the dark according to Drs. Jack A. Vernon (Princeton) and Thomas E. McGill (Williams College).

This does not hurt, This does not hurt,
This does not hurt,
Ow, Ow, ...ARE YOU KIDDING ME???

According to Dr. Seymour Hershman, co-author of "Medical and Dental Hypnosis," over 50,000 babies have been born in the U.S. to mothers who have hypnotized themselves to withstand the pain of childbirth.

1961

The U.S. battles a nationwide outbreak of Type A and Type B hepatitis.

A GOOD SUBJECT WITH A STiNK

The University of Chicago's Food Research Institute reveals that the moldy-looking coating of Limburger cheese contains a potent antibiotic that destroys an assortment of microbes and has probably saved many lives.

Putting An End To The *itch*

A live measles virus vaccine has been developed by Dr. John Enders in the Lederle Laboratories which the "Journal of the American Medical Association" calls "the newest and one of the greatest accomplishments in the history of public health."

buzz off!

Research has disclosed that stings from honeybees, bumblebees, yellow jackets, wasps and hornets are even more serious than believed before and can result in major allergic reactions such as skin eruptions, asthma and even death.

The Big Sneeze

At the 5th International Congress on Biochemistry, Chicago Medical School's Dr. Robert Goldfarb reports that after ten years of research, the protein causing allergic reactions in hay fever sufferers has been isolated from ragweed pollen.

NOTHING TO Sneeze at

A Columbia University physician reports good results in 86 out of the first 100 patients treated with a new spray for sinusitis called Phenyl-Drane.

FOOTLOOSE and FANCY FREE

Veterinarian Dr. D.M. Howard reports in the *Journal of the American Veterinary Medical Association* that he has successfully used artificial limbs to replace the accidentally severed hind feet of a dog.

As a result of fallout from Soviet nuclear tests, the U.S. reports an increase in radioactive iodine-131 in milk and fresh food in certain parts of America.

WHAT DID YOU SAY ?

Hearing tests conducted at the University of North Carolina reveal that temperature and humidity affect one's hearing as follows:

Most Acute:
Temperature: 50° F, Relative Humidity, 70%

Lowest Acuity:
Temperature: 20° F, Relative Humidity, 80%

Temperature: 90° F, Relative Humidity, 80%

90% of people who go on crash diets gain the lost weight back in six months.

TO PREVENT CRIPPLING, PHYSICAL AND OCCUPATIONAL THERAPY, INCLUDING ACTIVE EXERCISES DONE THROUGHOUT THE DAY, IS RECOMMENDED FOR EARLY TREATMENT OF RHEUMATOID ARTHRITIS.

A WEIGHTY PROBLEM:

The Metropolitan Life Insurance Company reports that 48 million Americans are overweight.

TIPS ON EATING

Enjoy and be happy eating.

Be aware of your reaction to certain foods.

Put diet control in the hands of your doctor.

Take your time eating and don't patronize restaurants with a fast turnover and a noisy atmosphere.

Avoid monotonous fad foods, crash diets and unbalanced irregular eating.

Speaking Of Eating

With a serious shortage of quality protein foods and food fats, the typical Russian diet consists of less than 3,000 calories daily made up of mostly carbohydrates including grains and potatoes, followed by animal protein, fats, oils and sugar.

PSYCHIATRISTS CONCLUDE

that neurotic fat people generally became emotionally unstable during childhood or adolescence and only intense therapy will lead to weight reduction and control as neurotic feelings of self-loathing are constantly being renewed every time they look into a mirror.

DROP THOSE FRENCH FRIES

Overweight children are more likely to become overweight adults than are normal or underweight children.

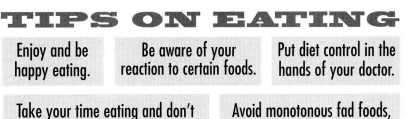

A young baboon by the name of **Cowboy** has been trained to push a button when he wants to eat requiring him to push the proper buttons about 200 to 300 times a day.

WHAT A YEAR IT WAS!

1961

RADIOISOTOPES

which are injected into the bloodstream are being tested in treating some forms of cancer.

CANCER

continues to be one of the primary causes of death after middle age.

HERE'S LOOKING AT YOU KID!

Researchers at New York's Presbyterian Hospital perform the first successful operation using an intense beam of light from a laser to treat a tumor in the eye of a human being.

GET OUT THAT SUNBLOCK

Evidence from experimental laboratory work supports the belief that exposure to the sun's ultra-violet rays is a primary factor in causing skin cancer.

U.S. Surgeon General **DR. LUTHER TERRY** announces that for the first time a chemical has killed a malignancy and holds out hope for future use of methotrexate which has been used on 63 women with cancer of the uterus resulting in 30 remissions.

DR. DENTON A. COOLEY of Houston's Baylor University is the first to surgically remove a blood clot from the lungs.

The National Multiple Sclerosis Society's **DR. THOMAS L. WILLMON** asserts that more cases of MS appear in the northern part of America than in the South with the same north-south ratio applying to Europe as well.

DR. CHARLES N. PEASE of Chicago's Children's Memorial Hospital warns that non-surgical methods used for scoliosis or curvature of the spine such as physical therapy, stretching, active and passive exercises are of no value and should be condemned because they offer false hopes.

At the 110th annual meeting, The American Medical Association delegates approve a resolution making it ethical for doctors to work with the nation's 13,500 osteopaths.

HERE'S SOMETHING TO MAKE YOU BURN

Statistics show that four out of five burn accidents occur in the home.

THERE'S NO PLACE LIKE HOME TO GET KILLED

The National Safety Council reports that falls kill and injure more people in the home than any other type of accident.

WELL SHUT MY MOUTH

Marking the first time the disease has appeared in Jordan, 400 serious cases of lockjaw are reported in the Red Sea port of Aqaba.

Dr. V.M. Hawthorne of Glasgow, Scotland warns that if your dog contracts tuberculosis, you could catch it from "man's best friend."

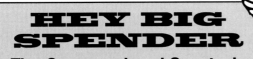

HEY BIG SPENDER

The Congressional Quarterly reports that the American Medical Association spent $146,894 in the first half of 1961, $80,000 more than the second biggest lobbyist, the AFL-CIO.

1961

There's Safety In Numbers

700 physicians and dentists in New York City form The Doctors' Association of the Department of Health, the first doctors' union in the U.S.

FACE-OFF

According to Dr. Samuel Ayres III of the University of California, a chemical face-peeling to remove wrinkles has merit if carried out by reputable doctors but warns that at least one death and severe scars in a number of women resulted from the procedure being performed by laypersons.

At the first National Congress on Medical Quackery sponsored by the AMA and FDA, attacks are made against the fraudulent practice of offering nutritional cure-alls in the form of vitamins and organic foods for everything from a variety of diseases to weight and cosmetic problems.

With between 16-17 million people now 65, an increased emphasis is being placed on the importance of motivation for the elderly including opposition to forced retirement as according to Ewald W. Busse's address at a conference on aging: "Medical science knows that people can die when they feel they have no purpose for living and no goal in life."

To make sure your legs get enough stimulation and to avoid a number of chronic bone conditions, Dr. Joseph T. Freeman says start climbing stairs again instead of using elevators and escalators.

New York's Sloan-Kettering Institute develops a simple blood test which reveals whether a patient is suffering from the early stages of disease and which internal organ is being affected.

1961 PSYCHOLOGICAL

If You Break Up With Me, I'm Taking The Razor

The sudden ending of a love affair or any great emotional upset can cause excessive hair growth on a woman's face because the stress can trigger the endocrine activity which stimulates hair production.

TELLTALE SIGNS OF A NEUROTIC WOMAN

Artificially colored platinum blond hair.

Coloring the grey hair.

Over-plucked and painted eyebrows (unless you're a model).

Wearing dark glasses when the sun isn't shining.

Bad teeth.

Ticklish stomach.

Unable to swallow pills.

Women are generally more generous in giving compliments to men than vice-versa and because they are eager to find a marriage partner, they are apt to view the opposite sex through rose-colored glasses.

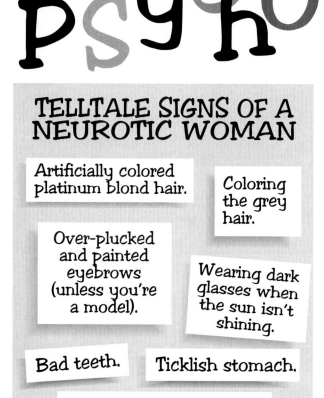

A New York psychiatrist has a theory that chronic, compulsive gamblers don't play to win, but in fact play to lose in order to prove they are not loveable by Lady Luck or by anyone else.

silence
IS LOUDER THAN WORDS

The theory of the "power of positive silence" has caught the attention of many psychologists, one of whom notes that a common use of silence is to express resistance or hostility. Other uses include silence with eyes opened wide which generally means antagonism and silence with closed eyes which generally indicates love and acceptance of another person.

LET IT ALL HANG OUT

An article appearing in STATE OF MIND stresses that being stoic in the face of personal tragedy is not necessarily a healthy virtue as bottling up one's feelings can lead to serious emotional, mental or physical ailments. Sobbing, anger or irritability are normal emotions when grieving and when these symptoms don't occur, it is recommended that medical help be sought.

90

PSYCHOLOGICAL PROFILES

...of a good SALESMAN

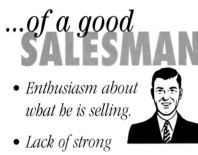

- *Enthusiasm about what he is selling.*

- *Lack of strong opinions on controversial matters and not idealistic.*

- *Personal desire for material success making it easier to convince others to buy.*

- *Ability to withstand any discomfort to make the sale.*

- *Knack for appearing warm and congenial when they really aren't.*

- *Although salesmen appear to be very sociable people, deep down most of the really successful ones are detached, lonely individuals.*

Columbia University psychologist Dr. James L. Malfetti asserts that a man drives a car the way he lives his life with the following profiles:

THE VIOLATOR:

- Young
- Aggressive
- Rebellious
- In conflict with others, including his family.

SAFE DRIVER:

- Pays his bills.
- Plans his vacations well in advance.
- Almost never gets into a fight.
- Gives the other driver the right of way.

San Francisco psychiatrist Dr. Francis J. Rigney asserts in his book The Real Bohemia that the Beatnik is a sad, mentally sick individual who needs psychiatric counseling.

SMARTY PANTS NEED NOT APPLY

If you're a genius, you won't be getting a job this summer with the Cleveland Recreation Department as the commissioner refuses to hire anyone with an IQ of over 140 on the grounds that they learn their job in a week and then lose interest.

With the increase in social pressures and status-seeking adults, more youngsters between the ages of 4 to 14 are suffering from peptic ulcers than ten years ago.

A study conducted of 900 patients under 17 years old admitted to New York's Bellevue Hospital indicates that 106 were there because of attempted suicide.

1961 Child Behavior

Asserting that children develop social interests when they are ready for them, Dr. Robert White of Harvard University warns that grown-ups who force a child to be sociable will probably wind up with a lonely member of a lonely crowd.

The desire for children to dress like members of the opposite sex does not necessarily lead to homosexuality but if they grow up and become transvestites, they can have relatively "normal" marriages if their partners are understanding of their proclivity such as a man wearing women's underwear under his suit or a woman wearing a necktie with her nightgown.

Psychoanalysts are discussing a new approach to therapy in which a parent and an adolescent child go into treatment together either privately or in small groups.

Dr. Benjamin Spock says that "next to the family, the most powerful force that molds a child's character is the school."

✓ College students who practice their religion are three times as likely to be opposed to premarital sex than their not-so-religious counterparts.

✓ Experts in family life observe that boys and girls are getting romantically interested in each other at younger and younger ages and that dating can begin in the fifth grade.

Youngster MONEY MATTERS

Following is the level of understanding of money at three different groups of children:

PRESCHOOL:

FOUR AND FIVE-YEAR OLDS begin to develop an awareness of money when you give them a few pennies in a store and help them choose something within that "budget."

HIGH SCHOOL:

Children of this age generally wish to be independent in money matters and insist on making their own spending decisions whether they have the judgment or not. They begin to learn about clothing and fabrics and discover that the cost of a garment is connected to material used and the quality of the tailoring.

GRADE SCHOOL:

SIX TO EIGHT-YEAR OLDS can usually distinguish the relationship between pennies, dimes, quarters and dollar bills and should be allowed to go to the store with a note to make simple purchases.

EIGHT AND NINE-YEAR OLDS can be taught the principles of saving.

TEN TO TWELVE-YEAR OLDS tend to be conformists and follow the crowd and the child who doesn't feel socially accepted by his peers will generally try to buy his way in by treating his classmates to ice cream or candy.

One in ten new mothers gets a case of post-delivery blues.

1961

Dr. Leopold Bellak of City Hospital in Elmhurst, New York predicts that the "Angry Young Men" and the "Beats" will probably be followed by a generation that won't even bother to get angry and that there will be a return to the "cocktail party" sociability.

A Psychotic By Any Other Name Is Still A Psychotic

Dr. Norbert Bromberg of the Albert Einstein College of Medicine in New York coins a new name for Adolf Hitler, "psychotic character," which differs from the true psychotic in one's ability to establish relations with people but like the true psychotic, has a relatively poor capacity to get along with others. Hitler's blind rages, violence, irrational hatred and paranoid ideas fall under the psychotic behavior description.

SCHIZOPHRENIA

The National Institute of Mental Health reveals that although schizophrenia is not hereditary, there is a greater than average chance that if one member of the family has the disease, others will as well.

The Joint Commission on Mental Illness and Health issues a report indicating that approximately one-half of the people in mental hospitals are schizophrenics with the majority of these patients being between 25 and 34 at time of admission.

Duke University conducts a study of the sexual activity of older married couples and finds that among the 70's to 80's age range, many are still sexually active having sex several times weekly with older males being more sexually active than females. The lower social classes continue to be active sexually into old age and engage in sex more frequently than those of upper social classes.

1961 New PRODUCTS AND INVENTIONS

An oddball invention is this vehicle being tested in Washington by the inventor himself.

Alas, the vehicle catches fire, but luckily the inventor is pulled to safety.

Well, er, it's not quite ready for the assembly line.

WHEN YOU SPEAK (anywhere) We Are LISTENING

A gigantic radio-telescope antenna capable of listening in on radio sources ten times farther into space is in operation 200 miles west of Sydney, Australia.

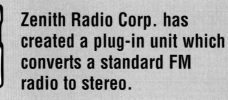

THERE'S A NEW SET OF EARS IN TOWN

New *Butterfly Wings* replace your old, reliable *Rabbit Ears* antennas on your television or FM radio.

Zenith Radio Corp. has created a plug-in unit which converts a standard FM radio to stereo.

GET OUT YOUR STOPWATCHES boys

United Airlines has installed a completely automated luggage-handling system at the new Los Angeles International Airport capable of retrieving baggage from an arriving plane and delivering it to the claims area in 2½ minutes.

WHAT A YEAR IT WAS!

Stink No More

Matchabelli introduces a combination deodorant-anti-perspirant called **Tact**.

1961

DALLAS' *Neiman-Marcus*

has installed a computer that offers gift suggestions.

SWALLOW THOSE WRINKLES AWAY

A New York dermatologist is testing a pill formulated by a major pharmaceutical house to remove crow's feet and wrinkles by putting moisture back into the skin.

COFFEE & CHEMICALS= YUMMY

Coffee-Mate introduces the first non-dairy creamer.

Oh Ken, We Love You

Barbie's friend **Ken** makes his debut.

slip slidin' away

Slip 'n Slide by Wham-O-Manufacturing hits the consumer market.

Hey, I heard that!

French scientists have developed a new electronic hearing aid small enough to fit inside the ear.

Swedish hospitals are using $.40 disposable paper blankets to replace woolen covers which are magnets for dust and germs.

CAN YOU TOP THIS?

Can-Top Machinery Corp. of Philadelphia has invented an easy-open top for cans which, when you give a little tug on the metal tab, lifts off the entire top.

CARVING UP THAT TURKEY, ELECTRIC STYLE

Minitone Electronics, Inc. is distributing an electric knife that makes carving and slicing meat a smooth operation.

KEEP THAT BATTERY HANDY

The world's first cordless power tool has been invented by **Black & Decker** and sells for around $50.

DRINK NOW – *THROW AWAY LATER*

International Latex Corp. has come out with a pre-sterilized disposable inner lining for baby bottles saving moms from having to wash and boil bottles.

BATHING YOUR BOVINES OR ... A MOO-ING EXPERIENCE

An automatic cow wash capable of washing 800 cows an hour is developed in California.

1961

THIS COULD MAKE YOUR HAIR CURL IF USED WHILE SHOWERING

Broxodent, a new electric toothbrush being manufactured by E.R. Squibb & Sons, has hit the market promising quick, easy brushing.

SHEDDING NEW LIGHT ON THE SUBJECT

A new dimmer with different light intensities is introduced by Electric-Solid Controls, Inc. of Minneapolis and will retail for **$24.95**.

DON'T TAKE THIS LIGHTLY

Flamescent, a shatterproof incandescent light bulb, has been developed by the Duro-Test Corporation, North Bergen, New Jersey.

A miniature gyroscope weighing less than a pound has been developed by the Sperry Gyroscope Co. of Great Neck, New York, paving the way for a vehicle to land on the moon within one mile of the targeted site.

HERE'S A JUICY TIDBIT

Fresh fruit and vegetable juices are yours with the flip of a switch with the new Osterizer electric juicer attachment.

BRINGING YOUR BEANS TO A GRINDING HALT

Out of West Germany comes a small electric coffee grinder which can grind coffee for eight to ten cups in ten seconds.

HEY HONEY, WOULD YOU SPRAY ME A GLASS OF MILK?

With two new technological developments, including DuPont's new gas called Freon C318, foods such as peanut butter or mayonnaise may be dispensed through aerosol cans.

GETTING OUT THE GREEN AND BLUE

Trading stamps will now be available at your local supermarket through the use of an automatic dispenser.

COULD YOU CALL MY WIFE AND TELL HER MY BOWLING GAME RAN LATE?

An emergency sun-powered **call box** tied into the police and fire departments is being tested on Los Angeles freeways.

KEEPING YOUR KID ON A LONG LEASH

The *Kiddy Kuf Leader* will prevent your toddler from toddling too far.

MAKE SURE YOU TAKE THE BABY OUT FIRST

A new collapsible baby carriage weighing 33 lbs. is designed in Holland.

GETTING THE OLD **HOT** FOOT

Keep those cold feet warm with new electrically heated socks being sold by Taylor Sales Co. of Wayne, PA.

BABY-SITTING MADE SIMPLE

On your next visit to grandma's house, along with your new collapsible baby carriage, take the new full-size compact portable crib that converts into a playpen.

DOES THIS TASTE SALTY TO YOU?

A new process for desalting seawater has been developed by the General Electric Co.

Just Singing In The Rain

Hum along with those raindrops

with a collapsible umbrella with a built-in transistor radio fresh off the boat from Tokyo.

WHAT A YEAR IT WAS!

1961

SHARK NO MORE

The Presto Shark Chaser, a shark-repellent kit originally developed for the Navy, is being marketed by Presto Dyechem of Yonkers, NY.

Swimming Upstream With A Paddle

James M. Wardle of Ottawa, Ontario, Canada has invented a "staircase" to help salmon rest as they hurdle over dams during their migration upstream to spawn.

THERE'S NOTHING FISHY HERE

You won't find your fish floating face up on your return from a holiday due to a new electric fish-feeder being marketed by Double "A" Brand of Chicago.

At Scripps Institution of Oceanography in La Jolla, California, tests are under way on a remote control vehicle designed to do the work of a diver on the ocean floor.

hello, dollies

New dolls making their debut in New York are *Hedda-Get-Bedda*, a doll with three rotating faces, and *Kissy*, who puckers up and makes kissing sounds when squeezed.

Parker
PEN COMPANY

introduces instant ink which is obtained by dipping a pre-filled capsule into water for 30 seconds.

NO FLASH IN THE PAN

Polaroid puts out its new models, J-66 and J-33, both of which are controlled by photoelectric mechanisms without numerical calibrations of any kind.

A new **FOOTBALL HELMET** has been designed by a neurosurgeon and two football coaches with the hope of cutting down on fatal head injuries.

THIS WON'T LEAVE YOU BREATHLESS

A joint venture between the Walter Kidde Co. Ltd. of England and the Scott Corp. of America has resulted in a new emergency oxygen breathing system for passengers flying in high altitude, pressurized cabin jet aircraft. The system is automatically activated if cabin pressure reaches 15,000 feet with the oxygen being dispensed through masks stored above the passengers' heads.

BagVertising

is created by Gaiber & Associates, Inc. of Chicago and you will soon see advertising messages on your supermarket shopping bags.

SHOPPING BAG

WHAT A YEAR IT WAS!

And For Those Confidential Love Notes

Holland is exporting a paper-shredding machine capable of chewing up 16 tons of paper in eight hours.

1961

LOOK WHAT JUST FLOATED IN

A new line of swimming pool furniture, including Aqua-Lounge, Aqua-Table and Aqua-Bar, are here in time for your summer fun.

While you're floating around on your new Aqua-Lounge have someone fix you a frozen daiquiri from Don the Beachcomber's new frozen fresh daiquiri mix.

A *Foreign Currency Dispenser* that accepts only $5 bills and exchanges them for Italian, French, German, Belgian or English currency has been installed at New York International Airport.

Designed by Mosler Safe Co. and engineered by International Telephone & Telegraph, the *Autobanker* system allows depositors to conduct banking transactions without ever leaving the comfort of their cars.

A new wireless microphone attached to a pocket-size transmitter has been introduced by Sony Corporation.

SMILE, YOU'RE ON CAMERA

A new rapid-sequence camera device mounted on a patrol car's dashboard will soon be aiding traffic enforcement.

A new device produced by Radatron, Inc. will sound a warning beep when you are approaching a police radar speed trap.

SMALLER IS BETTER

Jack Kilby of Texas Instruments invents the integrated circuit advancing ultra-miniature electronics.

To assist busy nursing staffs, an electronic medical device has been jointly developed by Minneapolis-Honeywell and the Mayo Clinic that automatically and scientifically measures and records temperature, pulse rate, respiration rate and diastolic and systolic blood pressure and sounds an alarm if a patient reaches a dangerous stage.

JUST WHEN YOU FOUND THOSE HOME KEYS

IBM unveils its new **Selectric** typewriter containing all type character symbols on a movable drum eliminating type bars and carriages.

LOOK MA, NO HANDS

General Motors enters the growing mobile two-way communications field marketing a hands-free car telephone.

Automatic dialing devices are being tested that contain a built-in directory of names and numbers most frequently dialed.

WHAT A YEAR IT WAS!

Patents have been issued on the following inventions:

- **An incinerator on wheels that burns garbage as it's collected.**

- **A vibrating mattress.**

- **A rocking platform for a bassinet.**

- **A collapsible picnic table and bench.**

- **Motorized water skis.**

- **Warning device that sounds when truck drivers exceed speed limits while going downhill.**

Dan C. Ross of Wappingers Falls, NY assigns IBM the rights to his patent on an automatic air traffic control system for tracking planes by transmitting pulsed signals sent from the planes to a central computer station on the ground.

The patent for an automatic check scanner is turned over to the General Electric Co. by its inventor **Dr. Kenneth R. Eldredge** of Stanford Research Institute.

PASSING
Creator of the Band-Aid, **Earl Dickson** dies at age 68.

WHAT'S NEW IN CARS

BUICK:
Introduces its *Skylark*, a flashy coupe with a more powerful engine.

RENAULT:
Front-wheel drive with cooling system sealed at the factory that never needs more water or antifreeze.

JAGUAR:
New *XK-E* series results in $30 million in orders at the International Auto Show in New York. Hardtop coupe: $6,320 Convertible: $5,795.

FROM CARTON TO COOLING...IN 77-SECONDS

INSTALL THIS FEDDERS AIR CONDITIONER YOURSELF
...SAVE $25-$35 IN LESS THAN A MINUTE AND A HALF!

Why wait for the air conditioning installer to get to your house when he's the busiest man in town? You can carry a summerful of comfort home with you tonight, start to enjoy it minutes after you get there...with a Series-77 Fedders Air Conditioner.

It comes with Fedders' do-it-yourself installation completely built-in, ready to slip into your window when it comes out of the factory shipping carton. Unlike other do-it-yourself air conditioners, there are no kits to buy...no separate parts to assemble ...no sill or sash fittings to install, when you choose a Fedders.

Following the authorized instructions packed with the air conditioner, you place it on the window sill... pull out flexible metal side panels... pull down window. Installation complete! It will stay there in your win-

dow safe and secure for years—or it can be moved in seconds for window cleaning or winter storage. You've seen it demonstrated on TV, so you *know* you can do it.

But stop at your Fedders dealer today for a closer look. Notice the miracle Weather Barrier that seals out rain, dust, heat...the one-piece design that eliminates leaky seams and separations...adjustable end flanges that accommodate to any type of double-hung window. There's a Series-77 Fedders for every room, every type of current and every budget. They all deliver family-size comfort.

Best of all, you'll save enough on installation and delivery charges to enable you to enjoy a genuine Fedders —the most widely owned, most confidently recommended Air Conditioner in the world.

PULL OUT SIDE PANELS   PULL DOWN WINDOW   INSTALLATION COMPLETE

FEDDERS
WORLD'S NO. 1 AIR CONDITIONER

100

ENTERTAINMENT

MOVIES

Movie producer **Otto Preminger** (right) casts English actor **Charles Laughton** (left) in the role of a South Carolina senator in the film *Advise and Consent.*

THEATRE

Broadway has its blackest season of the century with a total loss of $6 million with **Who's Afraid of Virginia Woolf** being the only hit. Playwrights voluntarily reduce their royalties and New York City removes its theatre tax.

All In A Day's Work, a new comedy series with **Dick Van Dyke** is in the works with TV comic **Carl Reiner** writing and producing.

TELEVISION

DANCE

LET'S TWIST AGAIN LIKE WE DID

Chubby Checker's *The Twist* is the dance at New York's Peppermint Lounge, the newest hangout for the café society crowd with the likes of **The Duke and Duchess of Bedford, Porfirio Rubirosa, Bill Zeckendorf, Jr., Judy Garland, Billy Rose, Tennessee Williams, William Inge, Norman Mailer** and **Greta Garbo** *showing up to shake their booties.*

1961 What's Playing AT THE MOVIES

A Majority Of One
A Raisin In The Sun
A Taste Of Honey
The Absent Minded Professor
All Hands On Deck
All In A Night's Work
Angel Baby
Atlantis, The Lost Continent
Babes In Toyland
Bachelor In Paradise
Black Pirate
Blue Hawaii
Breakfast At Tiffany's
By Love Possessed
Circle Of Deception
The Comancheros
Come September
Cry For Happy
david and goliath
The Devil At 4 O'Clock
El Cid
The Errand Boy
Flower Drum Song
Francis Of Assisi
Gidget Goes Hawaiian
Go Naked In The World
The Guns Of Navarone
The Honeymoon Machine
The Hoodlum Priest
The Hustler
The Innocents
Judgment At Nuremberg
Jules et Jim
King Of Kings
The Ladies' Man
Lafayette

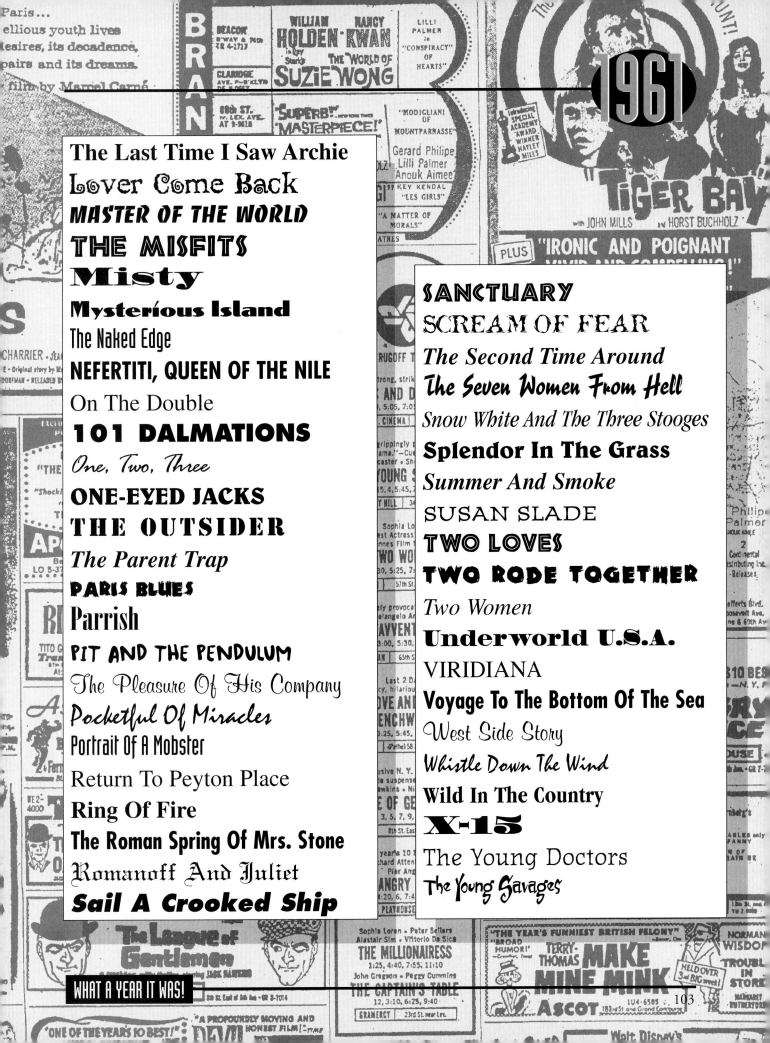

The Last Time I Saw Archie

Lover Come Back

MASTER OF THE WORLD

THE MISFITS

Misty

Mysterious Island

The Naked Edge

NEFERTITI, QUEEN OF THE NILE

On The Double

101 DALMATIONS

One, Two, Three

ONE-EYED JACKS

THE OUTSIDER

The Parent Trap

PARIS BLUES

Parrish

PIT AND THE PENDULUM

The Pleasure Of His Company

Pocketful Of Miracles

Portrait Of A Mobster

Return To Peyton Place

Ring Of Fire

The Roman Spring Of Mrs. Stone

Romanoff And Juliet

Sail A Crooked Ship

SANCTUARY

SCREAM OF FEAR

The Second Time Around

The Seven Women From Hell

Snow White And The Three Stooges

Splendor In The Grass

Summer And Smoke

SUSAN SLADE

TWO LOVES

TWO RODE TOGETHER

Two Women

Underworld U.S.A.

VIRIDIANA

Voyage To The Bottom Of The Sea

West Side Story

Whistle Down The Wind

Wild In The Country

X-15

The Young Doctors

The Young Savages

Glittering Celebrities Attend
Hollywood's Night Of The Oscars

Screen luminaries **Tony Curtis** and **Janet Leigh** (above right) and **Jean Simmons** (right) are among the celebrities on hand for Hollywood's annual bash.

Fans line up to catch a glimpse of their favorite movie star.

Tonight climaxes a year of hard work when the best efforts in motion picture production are rewarded.

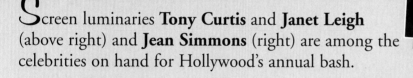

WHAT A YEAR IT WAS!

Eva Marie Saint presents the Oscar for Best Supporting Actor to **Peter Ustinov**, for his role in *Spartacus*, a spectacle that wins four awards for a major share of the night's honors.

Hugh Griffith presents **Shirley Jones** with the award for Best Supporting Actress for her role in *Elmer Gantry*.

For the first time in 33 years the Academy Awards ceremony is not held in Hollywood as this year the festivities take place in Santa Monica, California.

An excited **Greer Garson** gives the award for Best Actor to **Burt Lancaster** for *Elmer Gantry*.

Yul Brynner escorts the Best Actress of the Year, **Elizabeth Taylor**, who is convalescing from her recent grave illness.

Audrey **Hepburn** gives **Billy Wilder** a kiss on the cheek as she presents him with the Oscar for the year's Best Picture, *The Apartment*.

After four successive tries, Miss Taylor finally wins her Oscar and receives a long ovation from the audience.

1961

The Academy Awards

"And The Winner Is..."

Oscars Presented in 1961

BEST PICTURE
The Apartment

BEST ACTOR
BURT LANCASTER, *Elmer Gantry*

BEST ACTRESS
ELIZABETH TAYLOR, *Butterfield 8*

BEST DIRECTOR
BILLY WILDER, *The Apartment*

BEST SUPPORTING ACTOR
PETER USTINOV, *Spartacus*

BEST SUPPORTING ACTRESS
SHIRLEY JONES, *Elmer Gantry*

BEST SONG
"NEVER ON SUNDAY"
Never On Sunday

Elizabeth Taylor

1961 Favorites *(Oscars Presented In 1962)*

BEST PICTURE
West Side Story

BEST ACTOR
MAXIMILIAN SCHELL,
Judgment At Nuremberg

BEST ACTRESS
SOPHIA LOREN, *Two Women*

BEST DIRECTOR
ROBERT WISE, JEROME ROBBINS,
West Side Story

BEST SUPPORTING ACTOR
GEORGE CHAKIRIS, *West Side Story*

BEST SUPPORTING ACTRESS
RITA MORENO, *West Side Story*

BEST SONG
"MOON RIVER"
Breakfast At Tiffany's

Sophia Loren

WHAT A YEAR IT WAS!

New! Kodak automatic movie camera LESS THAN $50

Catch the moment-by-moment action with the new Kodak Automatic 8 Movie Camera.

Electric eye sets the lens! You just aim and shoot!

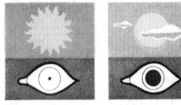

The new Kodak Automatic 8 Movie Camera has an electric eye that sets the exposure *automatically*.

Scene after scene, you take clear, rich color movies—without setting anything. The "expertness" has been built in. A fine $f/1.6$ lens gives you sharp detail. A built-in filter lets you take indoor or outdoor color movies on the same roll of film! Easy to load as a snapshot camera. Gets up to 40 average-length scenes on a single roll of film.

See this remarkable 8mm camera at your Kodak dealer's. It costs less than $50, or as little as $5 down at most dealers'. Ask your dealer for exact retail price.

Price is subject to change without notice.

The camera's electric eye works the way *your* eyes do. In bright sunlight, it closes down the lens. On dull or cloudy days, it opens the lens wider. It adjusts constantly so all your movies are correctly exposed.

...See all the new cameras in Kodak 1961 Cameraland—*at stores displaying the Kodak Girl*

EASTMAN KODAK COMPANY, Rochester 4, N.Y.

SEE KODAK'S "THE ED SULLIVAN SHOW" AND "OZZIE AND HARRIET"

107

MOVIES IN THE SKY

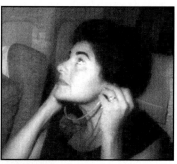

New high in entertainment is promised to airline passengers as **Walter Slezack** delivers a print of Universal International's *Come September*, the first regularly scheduled motion picture to be shown on an airplane.

The passengers lower their shades and get ready to watch the film starring **Rock Hudson, Gina Lollobrigida** and co-starring **Sandra Dee, Bobby Darin** and **Mr. Slezack**. It will be shown on five transcontinental trips and on flights to Europe.

The projector is hidden in the ceiling of the plane and each passenger has lightweight earphones.

Eating the requisite popcorn, this passenger's eyes are riveted to the screen as she watches screen idol **Rock Hudson**.

Walter Slezack has a coveted role in *Come September* and at this preview the actor has a chance to be his own critic. He seems satisfied with his performance.

Beautiful **Gina Lollobrigida** is sure to take the tedium out of any cross-country trip.

The film ends, these happy travelers give it an enthusiastic reception and Movies Aloft is now part of the flying experience.

WHAT A YEAR IT WAS!

Berlin Film Festival Awards

Best Feature	*La Notte* (Michelangelo Antonioni—Italy)
Best Documentary	*Description of a Struggle* (Israel)
Best Acting (Female)	Anna Karina *(Une Femme est Une Femme)* (France)
Best Acting (Male)	Peter Finch *(No Love For Johnny)* (England)

THE HARVARD LAMPOON AWARDS

Worst Picture: Butterfield 8

Worst Actor: Frank Sinatra (for his performance in *Can-Can*)

Worst Actress: Eva Marie Saint (for her performance in *Exodus*)

Most Drummed-Up Publicity Campaign: The Alamo

The New York Film Critics name *West Side Story* the best motion picture of the year making it the first musical to ever receive the award. *La Dolce Vita* is chosen best foreign film and **Sophia Loren** *(Two Women)* and **Maximilian Schell** *(Judgment at Nuremberg)* receive best actress and actor kudos. **Robert Rossen** gets best director nod for *The Hustler*.

The Directors Guild of America names **Billy Wilder** Director of the Year for his direction of *The Apartment*.

23-year old film actress Natalie Wood is immortalized as she becomes the 138th member of Hollywood to get her hands and feet carved in cement at **Grauman's Chinese Theatre**. The tradition began in 1927 with **Mary Pickford, Norma Talmadge** and **Douglas Fairbanks, Sr.** being the first stars to be so honored.

Dead since 1926, silent screen star **Rudolph Valentino** is honored with a huge marble monument in the famous son's hometown of Castellaneta, Italy.

BIG BUCKS AT THE BOX OFFICE

Tony Curtis
Doris Day
Sandra Dee
Cary Grant
William Holden
Rock Hudson
Jerry Lewis
Elvis Presley
Elizabeth Taylor
John Wayne

William Holden

TOMORROW'S BIG BUCKS AT THE BOX OFFICE

Warren Beatty
Horst Buchholz
Dolores Hart
Jim Hutton
Nancy Kwan
Carol Lynley
Hayley Mills
Paula Prentiss
Juliet Prowse
Connie Stevens

TOP GROSSING FILM OF THE YEAR

THE GUNS OF NAVARONE

FAMOUS BIRTHS

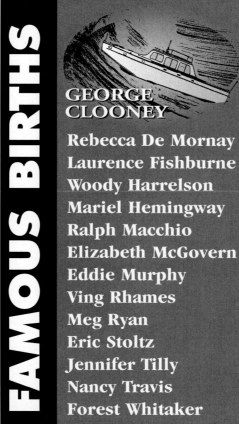

GEORGE CLOONEY

Rebecca De Mornay
Laurence Fishburne
Woody Harrelson
Mariel Hemingway
Ralph Macchio
Elizabeth McGovern
Eddie Murphy
Ving Rhames
Meg Ryan
Eric Stoltz
Jennifer Tilly
Nancy Travis
Forest Whitaker

CASTING CALL

Peter O'Toole

Young British Shakespearean actor, **Peter O'Toole**, is starring in **David Lean's** LAWRENCE OF ARABIA along with **Sir Alec Guinness**.

Warren Beatty makes his film debut in **Elia Kazan's** SPLENDOR IN THE GRASS.

Robert Montgomery's daughter **Elizabeth** is a new star at Paramount as she signs a long-term starring contract with her first role slated in NIGHT WITHOUT END.

Gene Tierney

Trying to recover her career after suffering a nervous breakdown, actress **Gene Tierney** shoots ADVISE AND CONSENT, her first film in seven years.

Audrey Hepburn and **Shirley MacLaine** star in **William Wyler's** remake of **Lillian Hellman's** THE CHILDREN'S HOUR, a story that deals with Lesbianism.

Swedish actor **Max von Sydow** has been cast in the role of Jesus Christ in THE GREATEST STORY EVER TOLD.

THE PRESIDENT ASKS FOR VETO POWER

President Kennedy asks for casting approval on the actor who is to portray him in the film version of his book "PT 109."

Motion picture producer **Samuel Goldwyn** is awarded $300,000 in damages against distributors of seven of his films — *The Best Years of Our Lives, The Secret Life of Walter Mitty, The Bishop's Wife, Enchantment, Roseanna McCoy, My Foolish Heart* and *A Song Is Born* — on the grounds that the distributors engaged in monopolistic practices that forced Goldwyn to take less than adequate compensation for the rights to show his films.

UNBANNING A BAN

Originally denied seals of approval because of their controversial stories, *The Moon Is Blue* (1953) whose subject is adultery, and *The Man With The Golden Arm* (1955) which deals with drug addiction, are both finally given the seal of approval by Hollywood's Production Code Administration.

• With advance sales of almost $300,000, **Fellini's** *La Dolce Vita* makes its U.S. premiere in a reserved seat showing in New York at $1.50 to $3.50 a seat.

• Warner Bros. offers $5.5 million for the film rights to *My Fair Lady*, the longest-running musical in Broadway history. **Audrey Hepburn** and **Cary Grant** are being considered for the Eliza Doolittle and Professor Higgins roles performed on Broadway by **Julie Andrews** and **Rex Harrison**.

Robert Alan Aurthur, Reginald Rose and Gore Vidal, three top American writers, form a production company to produce four motion pictures for Columbia over the next two years.

Passings

Handsome actor **Jeff Chandler**, star of *"Broken Arrow,"* *"Sign of the Pagan"* and a World War II veteran, dies after surgery at age 42.

Stage and screen star **Charles Coburn**, Best Supporting Actor Academy Award winner for his performance in *"The More the Merrier,"* dies at age 84 following minor surgery.

One of the great heroes of the silver screen, **Gary Cooper** succumbs to cancer less than a week after his 60th birthday. Former cartoonist, cowboy and movie extra, Cooper won two Academy Awards for Best Actor for his performances in *"Sergeant York"* and *"High Noon."* In addition to westerns, he also starred in gangster, war, comedy and adventure films.

A chorus girl in *"Ziegfeld Follies of 1917"* when she met William Randolph Hearst, actress **Marion Davies** (61) dies of cancer. Davies made millions from wise real estate investments, and had a widely-known long-term relationship with Hearst who built the luscious San Simeon estate for her.

Chico Marx, the piano playing, Italian-accented Marx Brother who starred with his younger brothers in such classic comedies as *"A Night At The Opera," "Duck Soup"* and *"Animal Crackers,"* dies of a heart ailment at age 70.

Twentieth Century Pictures co-founder and creator of "stars," **Joseph M. Schenck** dies at age 82.

Chinese-American actress **Anna May Wong**, former model and star of *"The Thief of Baghdad," "Old San Francisco"* and *"Portrait in Black,"* the latter made last year after a 17-year retirement, dies at age 54 of a heart attack.

1961

Andy Garcia arrives in the U.S. from Cuba.

THEY'RE ON THE ROAD AGAIN

Bob Hope and **Bing Crosby** get ready to shoot their seventh "Road" picture, THE ROAD TO HONG KONG, which will feature **Dorothy Lamour**.

MARLON, QUIT MUMBLING

In production throughout the year at a cost of $18,000,000, *MUTINY ON THE BOUNTY* becomes the most expensive film in history.

HE MOVES THOSE HIPS ALL THE WAY TO THE BANK

Despite lukewarm reviews, **Elvis Presley's** *BLUE HAWAII* is his most successful film spawning such hits as *Can't Help Falling in Love* and *The Hawaiian Wedding Song.*

Accompanied by her co-star **Montgomery Clift, Marilyn Monroe** is radiant as she attends a showing of *THE MISFITS* in New York.

Young Stanislavsky devotee, actor **John Cassavetes,** *releases* **SHADOWS,** *a $40,000 film shot without a script with his actors improvising a powerful although flawed piece of art.*

NEW SHOWS ON THE TV BLOCK
(A Sampling)

Alcoa Premiere
Ben Casey
The Bob Newhart Show
Bus Stop
Cain's Hundred
Car 54, Where Are You?
CBS Reports
David Brinkley's Journal
The Defenders
The Dick Powell Show
The Dick Van Dyke Show
Dr. Kildare
The DuPont Show Of The Week
87th Precinct
Father Of The Bride
Follow The Sun
Frontier Circus
The Hathaways
Hazel
International Showtime
The Joey Bishop Show
King Of Diamonds
Kraft Mystery Theater
Margie
The Mike Douglas Show
Mister Ed
Mrs. G. Goes To College
The New Breed
1, 2, 3 Go
Sing Along With Mitch
Straightaway
Target: The Corruptors
Window On Main Street
Yours For A Song

ABC revolutionizes sportscasting with the debut of its first Saturday afternoon **Wide World of Sports** with **Jim McKay**.

According to Nielsen research, *Americans are watching five hours and 22 minutes of television a day*.

Berating the violence and mediocrity in television programming, FCC Chairman **Newton N. Minow** tells more than 2,000 delegates to the National Association of Broadcasters convention in Washington that TV programming is *"a vast wasteland"* and that he did not intend *"to idly observe this squandering of the public's airwaves."*

NEW CARTOON SHOWS
The Alvin Show
The Bullwinkle Show
Calvin and the Colonel
Dick Tracy
Top Cat

FACES ON THE TUBE
(A Sampling)

Don Adams	Dorothy Kilgallen
Edie Adams	Don Knotts
Don Ameche	Ernie Kovacs
Morey Amsterdam	Michael Landon
Fred Astaire	Art Linkletter
Kaye Ballard	June Lockhart
Orson Bean	Paul Lynde
Ralph Bellamy	Fred MacMurray
Polly Bergen	Rose Marie
Milton Berle	E.G. Marshall
Shirley Booth	Groucho Marx
Walter Brennan	Jerry Mathers
Lloyd Bridges	Steve McQueen
Carol Burnett	Jayne Meadows
Raymond Burr	Mitch Miller
Edd "Kookie" Byrnes	Martin Milner
Pat Carroll	Garry Moore
Angela Cartwright	Mary Tyler Moore
Richard Chamberlain	Roger Moore
James Coburn	Harry Morgan
Chuck Connors	Audie Murphy
Robert Conrad	Leslie Nielson
Tim Conway	Jay North
Jackie Cooper	Bert Parks
Richard Crenna	Slim Pickens
Walter Cronkite	Tom Poston
Don DeFore	Ronald Reagan
William Demarest	Robert Reed
Bob Denver	Carl Reiner
John Derek	Michael Rennie
Troy Donahue	Tex Ritter
Hugh Downs	Wayne Rogers
Clint Eastwood	Cesar Romero
Ralph Edwards	Gena Rowlands
Shelley Fabares	Nipsey Russell
Nanette Fabray	Dick Sargent
Norman Fell	Telly Savalas
Henry Fonda	Rod Serling
Tennessee Ernie Ford	The Smothers Brothers
John Forsythe	Robert Stack
James Franciscus	Connie Stevens
Hermione Gingold	Elaine Stritch
Jackie Gleason	Renee Taylor
Gale Gordon	Robert Taylor
Lorne Greene	Marlo Thomas
Fred Gwynne	Richard Thomas
Buddy Hackett	Leslie Uggams
Pat Harrington, Jr.	Jack Warden
Florence Henderson	Dennis Weaver
Buck Henry	Adam West
Ronny Howard	Betty White
Tab Hunter	Jane Wyatt
Artie Johnson	Jane Wyman
Boris Karloff	Robert Young
Stubby Kaye	

WHAT'S PLAYING ON TV THIS WEEK

Adventures In Paradise
The Adventures
  Of Ozzie & Harriet
Alfred Hitchcock Presents
The Americans
The Andy Griffith Show
The Asphalt Jungle
Bachelor Father
Bonanza
Bronco
Candid Camera
Cheyenne
Concentration
The Danny Thomas Show
Dennis The Menace
The Detectives
  Starring Robert Taylor
The Dinah Shore Show
The Donna Reed Show
The Ed Sullivan Show
Father Knows Best
Five Star Jubilee
The Flintstones
Gunsmoke
Have Gun Will Travel
Hawaiian Eye
Hennesey
Holiday Lodge
I've Got A Secret
The Jack Benny Show
Laramie
Lassie
The Lawrence Welk Show

Leave It To Beaver
The Many Loves Of Dobie Gillis
Maverick
Meet The Press
My Three Sons
Naked City
National Velvet
One Happy Family
The Outlaws
The Perry Como Show
Perry Mason
Pete And Gladys
The Price Is Right
Rawhide
The Real McCoys
The Red Skelton Show
The Rifleman
Route 66
77 Sunset Strip
Surfside Six
Tales Of Wells Fargo
The Third Man
Thriller
To Tell The Truth
The 20th Century
The Twilight Zone
The Untouchables
Wagon Train
Walt Disney's Wonderful
  World Of Color
What's My Line
Whispering Smith

PROGRAMS THAT GET THE AX

Alcoa Presents
The Ann Sothern Show
The Barbara Stanwyck
  Show
Bat Masterson
The Deputy
Dick Powell's
  Zane Grey Theater
The Groucho Show
Guestward Ho!
Happy
Hong Kong
Ichabod And Me
The Life And Legend Of
  Wyatt Earp
The Loretta Young Show
Person To Person
Peter Gunn
Peter Loves Mary
Playhouse 90
Sea Hunt
The Shirley Temple Show
The Spike Jones Show
Stagecoach West
The Steve Allen Show
Sugarfoot
The Tab Hunter Show
This Is Your Life

The Peacock Wags Its Tail For You

NBC offers more than 1,600 hours of color broadcasting this year, up approximately 600 hours over last year.

NBC launches its **Saturday Night at the Movies**, the first series broadcasting Hollywood films made after 1948 and the first to be shown in color.

Walt Disney switches his black-and-white program from ABC to NBC and re-titles it **Walt Disney's Wonderful World of Color**.

Having given up television manufacturing five years ago, **General Electric** resumes making color television sets.

An estimated 30 million people watch Alan Shepard, Jr.'s suborbital flight at 9:34 a.m. EST, making it the largest television audience in history.

The National Association of Broadcasters amends the code for TV stations to prohibit the carrying of more than two consecutive commercials during evening network station breaks.

AND NOW IT'S TIME FOR A LONGER COMMERCIAL BREAK

ABC is the first network to launch a 40-second local station break to allow the airing of more commercials.

MOVE OVER, KING KONG

The Federal Communications Commission gives the nod to a 3-year trial for the nation's first subscription television and installs a UHF transmitter on top of the Empire State Building.

Puppeteers **Jim Henson** and **Frank Oz** create the inimitable **Miss Piggy**.

HELLO, CHARLIE

Sporting a beret and dark glasses, Beatnik **Charlie the Tuna** makes his television debut touting the merits of Star Kist Tuna.

Making his debut on British television, **Mort Sahl** is characterized as "half a wit" by the critics.

The Special Freedom and Leadership Award goes to radio and television personalities **Dave Garroway** and **Arthur Godfrey**.

WELL! WHAT A DEAL!

Jack Benny sells his J & M Productions, Inc. to Music Corp. of America exchanging the stock he and his wife **Mary Livingston** own for 45,000 shares of MCA valued at almost $3 million on the New York Stock Exchange.

George Bernard Shaw's *Candida* makes its American TV debut in Los Angeles on KNXT-TV.

Ed Sullivan criticizes the low-cut dress **Zsa Zsa Gabor** wears on **The Bob Hope Show** filmed at Guantanamo Bay saying that she doesn't set an *"inspiring example for our youngsters in the service."*

PASSING

Star of *"I Married Joan,"* comedienne **Joan Davis**, who also worked in vaudeville, the movies and at one time had a radio show, dies at age 48.

WHAT A YEAR IT WAS!

115

1961

Astaire Time

Gunsmoke

Have Gun Will Travel

The Ed Sullivan Show

The Untouchables

Playhouse 90

My Three Sons

Rawhide

The Lawrence Welk Show

Wagon Train

Candid Camera

EMMY awards

SERIES

HUMOR	*The Jack Benny Show*
DRAMATIC	*Macbeth*
VARIETY	*Astaire Time*

PERFORMERS

ACTOR	**Raymond Burr**
	Perry Mason
ACTRESS	**Barbara Stanwyck**
	The Barbara Stanwyck Show
VARIETY	**Fred Astaire**
	Astaire Time

Rod Serling wins an Emmy Award for writing for **The Twilight Zone**.

FAMOUS BIRTHS

Julia Louis Dreyfus

Michael J. Fox

Peri Gilpin

Heather Locklear

James Gandolfini

Educational television transmitted into the classroom begins in selected schools in Indiana, Illinois, Wisconsin, Michigan, Ohio and Kentucky.

A documentary on Soviet influence in Africa called "The Red and the Black" airs on ABC.

WHAT A YEAR IT WAS!

FROM RCA VICTOR

NEW VISTA TV

See all the RCA Victor New Vista TV models in all their beauty—all with the revolutionary New Vista Tuner!

RCA VICTOR sets a new standard for picture quality —engineered for the <u>clearest</u>, <u>steadiest</u> <u>picture</u> ever!

The Most Trusted Name in Television
RADIO CORPORATION OF AMERICA

New Vista TV is the picture of quality for these basic reasons:

1. Automatic build-up of weak signals! Amazing New Vista tuner has extra pulling power, brings in sharper, steadier pictures in many difficult reception areas. On all models.

2. One-set fine tuning! Tune once for best reception—and the set remembers! Many models.

3. Glare-proof picture tube! Cuts glare and reflection. Easy to clean. Many models.

4. Automatic scene control! The too-dark scenes are brightened, the too-brilliant scenes are darkened . . . automatically. All models.

5. New RCA Victor Magic Eye: Automatically adjusts brightness and contrast for the best picture reception regardless of changes in room lighting. A feature on many models.

6. RCA Victor's Wireless Wizard turns the set *completely* off. Lets you change channel and even the volume! Many models.

7. Automatic interference barriers! Reduce man-made interference, keep picture steady when you switch channels, and at proper height through operating temperature changes. All models.

See Walt Disney's new series, "The Wonderful World of Color" starting Sunday, Sept. 24, NBC-TV Network.

117

1961 RADIO

The most notable innovation this year is frequency modulation (FM) stereophonic broadcasting.

NO. OF AM STATIONS: 3,609
NO. OF FM STATIONS: 896

Ratings jump 28% as KMOX Radio, a St. Louis CBS affiliate, continues its pioneering format of news, interviews with interesting people and listener questions, now for seven hours a day. Other CBS stations in Boston, Los Angeles, New York and Philadelphia pick up the format.

Famous Births
Gary Dell'Abate
Melanie Mitchell

PASSING

Inventor of over 300 inventions including the audion tube which allowed for the creation of radio, television and movies, **Lee De Forest** dies at age 87. A pioneer in wireless communications and considered the father of radio, De Forest presented the first radio news broadcast.

President Kennedy authorizes live broadcasts of his press conferences on both radio and television.

The Radio-Television News Directors Association honors President Kennedy as "the man who has contributed most to the advancement of broadcast news."

On the radio since 1952, the popular **GUNSMOKE** program goes off the air.

LAUGHING MATTERS

Phyllis Diller is appearing at Greenwich Village's Bon Soir.

Mort Sahl entertains patrons at New York's Basin Street East.

Young **Dick Gregory** is the first black comedian to hit the big time in the nightclub circuit.

Television clown **Sid Caesar** is playing to a packed audience at New York's Copacabana club where he's doing his first club date since 1950.

1961 Popular Songs

A Hundred Pounds Of Clay . . *Gene McDaniels*
Ain't That Just Like A Woman . *Fats Domino*
Blue Moon . . . . *The Marcels*
Breakin' In A Brand New
  Broken Heart . . . . *Connie Francis*
Calendar Girl . . . . *Neil Sedaka*
Calcutta . . . . *Lawrence Welk*
Cinderella . . . . *Paul Anka*
Crazy . . . . *Patsy Cline*
Crying . . . . *Roy Orbison*
Daddy's Home . . . . *Shep &
                                          The Limelites*
Dance On Little Girl . . . . *Paul Anka*
Dedicated To The One I Love . *The Shirelles*
Everlovin' . . . . *Ricky Nelson*
Every Beat Of My Heart . . . . . *Gladys Knight
                                          And The Pips*
Flaming Star . . . . *Elvis Presley*
Fool #1 . . . . *Brenda Lee*
Frankie And Johnny . . . . *Brook Benton*
Good Time Baby . . . . *Bobby Rydell*
Goodbye Cruel World . . . . . . *James Darren*
Happy Birthday, Sweet Sixteen . *Neil Sedaka*
Hello Mary Lou . . . . *Ricky Nelson*
Hit The Road Jack . . . . *Ray Charles*
I Fall To Pieces . . . . *Patsy Cline*
I Just Don't Understand . . . . . *Ann-Margret*
I Like It Like That . . . . *Chris Kenner*
I'll Never Smile Again . . . . . . *The Platters*
I'm Comin' On Back To You . . *Jackie Wilson*
It Keeps Rainin' . . . . *Fats Domino*
Lazy River . . . . *Bobby Darin*
Let's Twist Again . . . . *Chubby Checker*
Letter Full Of Tears . . . . *Gladys Knight
                                          And The Pips*
The Lion Sleeps Tonight . . . . . *The Tokens*
Little Devil . . . . *Neil Sedaka*
Little Sister . . . . *Elvis Presley*
Mama Said . . . . *The Shirelles*
Michael . . . . *The Highwaymen*
Nature Boy . . . . *Bobby Darin*
Never On Sunday . . . . *The Chordettes*

One Mint Julep . . . . *Ray Charles*
Please Mr. Postman . . . . *The Marvelettes*
Please Tell Me Why . . . . *Jackie Wilson*
Pretty Little Angel Eyes . . . . . *Curtis Lee*
Quarter To Three . . . . *Gary "U.S." Bonds*
Raindrops . . . . *Dee Clark*
Rock-A-Bye Your Baby
  With A Dixie Melody . . . . . *Aretha Franklin*
Runaround Sue . . . . *Dion*
Runaway . . . . *Del Shannon*
September In The Rain . . . . . *Dinah Washington*
Shop Around . . . . *Smokey Robinson
                                          And The Miracles*
Some Kind Of Wonderful . . . *The Drifters*
Stand By Me . . . . *Ben E. King*
Take Five . . . . *Dave Brubeck
                                          Quartet*
Take Good Care Of My Baby . *Bobby Vee*
Temptation . . . . *The Everly Brothers*
Together . . . . *Connie Francis*
Tonight My Love, Tonight . . . *Paul Anka*
Transistor Sister . . . . *Freddy "Boom-
                                          Boom" Cannon*
Travelin' Man . . . . *Ricky Nelson*
True, True Love . . . . *Frankie Avalon*
The Watusi . . . . *The Vibrations*
The Way You Look Tonight . . *The Lettermen*
What A Party . . . . *Fats Domino*
What'd I Say . . . . *Jerry Lee Lewis*
Where The Boys Are . . . . *Connie Francis*
Who Put The Bomp In The
  Bomp, Bomp, Bomp . . . . . . *Barry Mann*
Will You Love Me Tomorrow? . *The Shirelles*
You Must Have Been A
  Beautiful Baby . . . . *Bobby Darin*

119

Fisher

After not singing for over a year, crooner **Eddie Fisher** steps up to the microphone in a comeback show at the Desert Inn in Las Vegas with his wife **Liz Taylor** at ringside along with her physician.

Judy Garland gives what is considered to be the greatest concert of her career at Carnegie Hall and her two-disc "Judy Garland At Carnegie Hall" tops the charts for 13 weeks.

Sammy Davis, Jr. has a glittering opening night in London of his one-man show sans his wife **May Britt** who stays home to take care of their baby who has a cold.

Marilyn Monroe shows up for **Frank Sinatra's** midnight opening at the Sands Hotel in Las Vegas fanning rumors that they are an item.

Sinatra

NEW TO THE RECORDING SCENE

Glen Campbell
Judy Collins
Ben E. King
Gladys Knight And The Pips
The Lettermen
Tony Orlando
Gene Pitney
Paul Revere & The Raiders
Del Shannon
The Spinners
Ray Stevens
The Tokens
Mary Wells

NO MORE PAY NOW, PLAY LATER

Payola charges against five record distributors including Columbia Record Distributors, Inc. and Columbia Records Sales Corp. of New York, Interstate Electric Co. of New Orleans and Capital Records Distributing Corp. and Dot Records, Inc. of Hollywood are dismissed by the FTC.

A-ONE, AN-A-TWO

Lawrence Welk receives his first gold record for *Calcutta* after 32 years of recording pop singles, and it's presented to him in a brown paper sack while he's having lunch at Hollywood's Brown Derby.

The Red Garter is one of the hottest bars in San Francisco where fans show up nightly to drink beer while they listen to banjos accompanied by drums, tuba, piano and even musical saws.

Famous Births

Boy George

Melissa Etheridge

k.d. lang

Wynton Marsalis

120

1961 ADVERTISEMENT

121

1961

GRAMMY awards

Song Of The Year	*Moon River* Johnny Mercer, songwriter Henry Mancini, composer
Record Of The Year	*Moon River* Henry Mancini
Album Of The Year	*Judy At Carnegie Hall* Judy Garland
Best Rock 'n' Roll Recording	*Let's Twist Again* Chubby Checker
Best Rhythm & Blues Recording	*Hit The Road Jack* Ray Charles
Best Jazz Performance, Big Band	*West Side Story* Stan Kenton
Best Country & Western Performance	*Big Bad John* Jimmy Dean
Best Folk Performance	*The Belafonte Folk Singers At Home And Abroad* The Belafonte Folk Singers
Best Spoken Word Recording	*Humor In Music* Leonard Bernstein
Best Comedy Recording	*An Evening With Mike Nichols And Elaine May* Mike Nichols & Elaine May
Best Soundtrack Album - Original Cast	*West Side Story*
Best Soundtrack Album - Score	*Breakfast At Tiffany's*

Folksy Corner

What Did You Say He Said?

BOB DYLAN, a rather disheveled young, talented man with a compelling stage presence, makes his debut at the hallowed Gerde's Folk City in New York's Greenwich Village.

20-year old folk singer **JOAN BAEZ** completes her first extended tour which focuses primarily on college campuses and her first two solo albums released by Vanguard enjoy immediate hit status.

The Day The Singing Died

Objecting to folk singers on the grounds that they are an undesirable element, the collective folk voice generally heard in Greenwich Village's Washington Square is silenced after a decree by Park Commissioner, liberal Republican Newbold Morris, that there would be no more singing.

Here's Tommy And Dickie

THE SMOTHERS BROTHERS are appearing at the posh Blue Angel where their satirical folk music and brotherly banter is sure to make you laugh.

OY COULD THAT LADY SING

MAHALIA JACKSON performs her gospel music to a packed, mesmerized audience in Tel Aviv's main auditorium.

Jackson

Three tunes written by **WILLIE NELSON** hit the charts — *Crazy*, *Funny How Time Slips Away* and *Hello Walls*.

122

WHAT A YEAR IT WAS!

Alto Sax

FIRST	*Julian "Cannonball" Adderly*
SECOND	*Johnny Hodges*

Tenor Sax

FIRST	*John Coltrane*
SECOND	*Coleman Hawkins*

Baritone Sax

FIRST	*Gerry Mulligan*
SECOND	*Harry Carney*

Clarinet

FIRST	*Buddy DeFranco*
SECOND	*Edmund Hall*
	Pee Wee Russell

A RECORD NUMBER OF RECORDS

600 jazz albums are released this year, a record number.

Dizzy Gillespie performs two new important jazz suites at the Monterey Jazz Festival written by Argentine pianist, Lalo Schifrin.

HOW HIGH THEIR MOONS

Peggy Lee, Ella Fitzgerald, Nat "King" Cole and *Frank Sinatra* reach new peaks of success with the general public.

Beatniks rub elbows with uptown jazz lovers as they show up for saxophonist *John Coltrane's* opening at New York's Village Gate.

Thelonious Monk and his quartet perform at the Museum of Modern Art playing such favorites as *Getting Sentimental Over You, Sweet and Lovely* and *Sweet Georgia Brown.*

Leading his 18-piece orchestra at New York City's Freedomland amusement center, BENNY GOODMAN *(right)* **brings back the good old sounds of yesterday, playing his famous theme** *Let's Dance*.

SONNY ROLLINS *(left)* **is playing his tenor sax at the Jazz Gallery in New York.**

BUT CAN SHE SHIMMY LIKE HER SISTER KATE?

Likened to swiveling her hips like Elvis, 20-year old Swedish-born singer Ann-Margret Olson, known as **Ann-Margret**, has one of the fastest-moving singles on the charts called *I Just Don't Understand* and is well on her way to becoming a major sex symbol.

The Shirelles are the first female rock 'n' roll group to hit the #1 spot with their recording of Gerry Goffin and Carole King's song *Will You Love Me Tomorrow?*

Gary "U.S." Bonds holds the best-selling record position for three weeks with his raucous rock 'n' roll recording of *Quarter To Three.*

The First International Festival of Rock 'n' Roll, including an American soloist and a U.S. Air Force orchestra, is held at the Palais des Sports in Paris.

ANKA'S AWEIGH

Teenage idol, 19-year old songwriter **PAUL ANKA**, who packs the audiences in wherever he performs, faces a hysterical mob at the new Woolworth store in San Juan, Puerto Rico and has to be carried out by police over the heads of his screaming fans and whisked away in a helicopter.

Earning almost as much as the combined salaries of the President and Vice President of the United States and half the U.S. Senate and regarded as a phenomenon of our time, **PAUL ANKA** performs to an overflow crowd at the Copacabana, performing some of the 125 tunes he's written including *Diana.*

Berry Gordy's Motown Records scores its first #1 hit with *Please Mr. Postman.*

Classical Music

Breaking his vow to never play in a country that recognizes Franco's Spain, famed cellist **PABLO CASALS** plays for President John F. Kennedy in a one-hour concert at the White House with a glittering audience of the top composers and conductors of the nation in attendance.

IGOR STRAVINSKY, militant anti-Communist whose music has been banned in the Soviet Union since 1924, is asked to return to his homeland for a celebration honoring his 80th birthday. The delegation of Russian composers tells Stravinsky that his music is once again being played and with great emotion he agrees to visit Russia for the first time since he left in 1914.

Stravinsky

BESSKY YOU BE MY WOMANSKY

GEORGE GERSHWIN'S *Porgy and Bess gets its first Russian-language performance in a Moscow theatre.*

With New York Philharmonic ticket sales the highest in history, its conductor **Leonard Bernstein** is awarded a new seven-year contract — the longest since the turn of the century.

Leonard **Bernstein** establishes the Leonard Bernstein Music Scholarship Endowment at Brandeis University.

Vienna-born **Eric Leinsdorf** is slated to take over the conductor's baton of the Boston Symphony from its present director **Charles Munch** who is retiring in 1962.

Composer **Arthur Rubinstein** receives the Royal Philharmonic Society of London Gold Medal.

27-year old **Agustin Anievas** wins the Gold Medal and $5,000 first prize in the first Dimitri Mitropoulos International Music Competition at the finals held in New York City.

THEY'RE ON THE ROAD AGAIN

• The New York Philharmonic makes a 19,000-mile tour including Japan, Alaska and Canada.

• The Santa Fe Opera goes to Berlin and Belgrade.

• The Warsaw Philharmonic and Berlin Philharmonic visit America.

Isaac Stern joins **Jack Benny** in Bach's *Concerto in D Minor for Two Violins* in "Carnegie Hall Salutes Jack Benny."

Carl Sandburg records a poetry album for children called *Carl Sandburg's Poems for Children* and Capital Records releases *The Fanciful World of Ogden Nash*, also a poetry album for children.

20,000 PEOPLE CRAM NEW YORK'S LEWISOHN STADIUM TO HEAR A CONCERT BY VAN CLIBURN.

Pulitzer Prize
for Music

Symphony No. 7
Walter Piston
First performed by the Philadelphia Orchestra on February 10, 1961

PASSING

A cerebral thrombosis takes the life of 81-year old conductor and composer **Sir Thomas Beecham**, who founded his own opera company and the London Philharmonic, brought Russian ballet and opera to Britain and was revered for his sarcastic wit.

WHAT A YEAR IT WAS!

Leopold Stokowski gets an explosive standing ovation as he makes his debut conducting at the Metropolitan Opera.

The Harvest by **Vittorio Giannini** is produced by The Lyric Opera of Chicago.

Blood Moon by **Norman Dello Joio** is produced by the San Francisco Opera.

The Met presents **Puccini's Turandot** for the first time in 31 years.

Puccini

Following the death of her mother two days before, soprano **Joan Sutherland** makes her local debut in New York's Town Hall in the American Opera Society's production of **Bellini's Beatrice di Tenda**.

Diva **Maria Callas** takes 25 curtain calls following her performance in **Medea** at Milan's La Scala only five days after undergoing painful treatment for sinusitis.

Celebrated Swedish movie director **Ingmar Bergman** will stage his first opera in Stockholm— **Stravinksy's The Rake's Progress**.

West Berlin opens its new $7,000,000 Deutsche Oper replacing the opera house destroyed in World War II.

New Operas

Elegy For Young Lovers
Hans Werner

Lavinia
Henri Barraud

Uno Sguardo Dal Ponte
Renzo Rosselini
(Based on Arthur Miller's
A View From The Bridge)

Intoleranza
Luigi Nono

The American Opera Project of the Ford Foundation:

The Wings Of The Dove
Douglas Moore
(Based on the novel by
Henry James)

The Crucible
Robert Ward
(Based on the play by
Arthur Miller)

A labor dispute between the New York Metropolitan Opera and the AFL-CIO Federation of Musicians threatens to close down the season but Labor Secretary Arthur J. Goldberg helps get the two parties to agree to arbitration.

Despite a wave of protests received by sponsors of the Wagner Festival in Bayreuth, West Germany for the casting of a black performer, St. Louis mezzo-soprano **Grace Bumbry** wins critical acclaim for her performance as Venus in *Tannhauser*.

Leontyne Price debuts in the Metropolitan Opera's production of *Il Trovatore*, making her the first black American to star at the Met on opening night.

Having sung *Aida* at some of the greatest opera houses in the world, **Leontyne Price** finally gets to sing it for the first time at the Met.

WHAT A YEAR IT WAS!

Dance

Maria Tallchief dances *Miss Julie* with the *Royal Danish Ballet.*

ANOTHER "COVER-UP" FOR THE VICE SQUAD

NOTICE IS GIVEN TO THE BILTMORE THEATER THAT THE FEMALE DANCERS OF **LES BALLETS AFRICANS** WILL NOT BE ALLOWED TO APPEAR NUDE FROM THE WAIST UP AND ARE ORDERED TO WEAR BRAS.

RUSSIA NO! PARIS, OUI!

Pleading for protection, Russian ballet star of the Kirov Ballet group of Leningrad, 23-year old **Rudolf Nureyev**, defects from the troupe as they are about to board a plane in Paris for London and promptly joins France's Marquis de Cuevas' ballet troupe where he performs *Sleeping Beauty* only one week after his defection.

• The Kirov Ballet performs in London and makes its American debut at New York's Metropolitan Opera House.

• Russia's folk-dance troupe, Moiseyev Dance Company, opens its second American and Canadian tour to thunderous applause.

• 50 members of Moscow's Bolshoi Ballet including **Maya Plissetskaya** and the legendary **Galina Ulanova** dance in the United Arab Republic.

• The American Ballet Theatre returns to the U.S. after completing successful appearances in the Soviet Union.

• The Royal Ballet, featuring prima ballerina **Margot Fonteyn**, makes its debut in the Soviet Union.

In preparation for the summer tour of Europe, **Jerome Robbins** reorganizes his Ballets: U.S.A.

•

Jerome Robbins' Ballets: U.S.A. dances at the Festival of Two Worlds in Spoleto, Italy.

•

EVENTS, Jerome Robbins' new ballet based on homosexuality, racial prejudice, apathy, anxiety and fear, receives poor reviews from the critics.

•

Martha Graham introduces two new works, **ONE MORE GAUDY NIGHT** and **VISIONARY RECITAL**, based on Antony and Cleopatra and Samson and Delilah respectively.

Over 1,000 people show up at Manhattan's Palladium Ballroom to dance the newest dance craze sweeping the U.S. and Europe, LA PACHANGA. Roseland bars the dance fearing its floor would collapse.

The CHA-CHA still enjoys international popularity and there is a revival of the FISH.

• *American Dance* is featured at The Boston Arts Festival chronicling 50 years of dance in America.

• **The National Ballet of Canada** celebrates its tenth anniversary.

• **The New York City Ballet** presents the premiere performance of *Modern Jazz: Variants* backed by **The Modern Jazz Quartet** and the orchestra of the **New York City Ballet** thus combining jazz and symphonic music.

• Kansas-born **Remi Gassmann** creates an eerie electronic score for **George Balanchine's** new ballet entitled *Electronics*.

PASSING

Ziegfeld Follies star **Annabelle Whitford Buchan** dies at age 92.

WHAT A YEAR IT WAS!

ON BROADWAY

ANOTHER OPENING, ☆ ANOTHER NIGHT

A MAN FOR ALL SEASONS

CARNIVAL

COME BLOW YOUR HORN

HOW TO SUCCEED IN BUSINESS WITHOUT REALLY TRYING

MARY, MARY

Paul Scofield in *A Man For All Seasons*

ON BROADWAY

A Call On Kuprin

A Cook For Mr. General

A Far Country

A Shot In The Dark

Big Fish, Little Fish

The Caretaker

The Comedie Française

The Complaisant Lover

Daughter Of Silence

The Devil's Advocate

Donnybrook!

Everybody Loves Opal

Gallows Humor

The Gay Life

The Happiest Girl In The World

The Importance Of Being Oscar

Kean

Let It Ride!

Luther

Mandingo

Milk And Honey

Purlie Victorious

Rhinoceros

Show Girl

Sunday In New York

13 Daughters

Julie Harris in
A Shot In The Dark

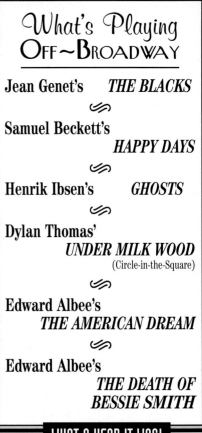

What's Playing Off~Broadway

Jean Genet's **THE BLACKS**

Samuel Beckett's **HAPPY DAYS**

Henrik Ibsen's **GHOSTS**

Dylan Thomas' **UNDER MILK WOOD**
(Circle-in-the-Square)

Edward Albee's **THE AMERICAN DREAM**

Edward Albee's **THE DEATH OF BESSIE SMITH**

WHAT A YEAR IT WAS!

1961

Jason Robards, Jr. (left) and Hume Cronyn in *Big Fish, Little Fish*

For the first time in ten years, **IRVING BERLIN** is hard at work on a Broadway musical called *Mr. President*.

WAY TO GO, DAVID!!

Disgusted with negative theatre reviews, producer **David Merrick** rounds up ordinary people with the same names as the critics and prints their "rave reviews."

RICHARD RODGERS and **ALAN JAY LERNER** team up to write a Broadway musical.

32-year old cartoonist **Jules Feiffer** *writes his first piece for the stage, a revue called* **The Explainers**, *which is playing at Chicago's new Playwrights Cabaret Theatre.*

Humorist **James Thurber** *is the only American to join the London West End production of his* **A Thurber Carnival**.

Gene Wilder *makes his Broadway debut.*

Peter Fonda, *Henry's son, makes his Broadway debut in* **Blood, Sweat And Stanley Poole**.

Members of Actors' Equity Association will no longer perform in segregated theatres.

Sir Laurence Olivier *plays against* **Anthony Quinn** *in the Broadway production of Anouilh's* **Becket**.

PASSING

The final curtain goes down on **George S. Kaufman** and **Moss Hart**, partners on such Broadway hits as *"The Man Who Came To Dinner"* and the Pulitzer Prize winning *"You Can't Take It With You."* Former Algonquin Round Table member Kaufman, who also won a Pulitzer for *"Of Thee I Sing,"* dies at age 71. Hart, who received a Tony Award for directing *"My Fair Lady,"* and wrote the best-selling book *"Act One,"* dies at age 57, six months after Kaufman.

WHAT A YEAR IT WAS!

129

Tony Awards
1961

PLAY
"Becket"
Jean Anouilh (playwright)

MUSICAL
"Bye Bye Birdie"

DRAMATIC ACTOR
Zero Mostel
"Rhinoceros"

DRAMATIC ACTRESS
Joan Plowright
"A Taste Of Honey"

DIRECTOR
Sir John Gielgud
"Big Fish, Little Fish"

MUSICAL ACTOR
Richard Burton
"Camelot"

MUSICAL ACTRESS
Elizabeth Seal
"Irma La Douce"

NEW YORK DRAMA CRITICS' CIRCLE AWARD

BEST PLAY	ALL THE WAY HOME
BEST FOREIGN PLAY	A TASTE OF HONEY
BEST MUSICAL	CARNIVAL!

SPECIAL TONYS

The Theatre Guild for organizing the first repertory company to go abroad for the State Department.

David Merrick in recognition of a fabulous production record over the past seven years.

Composer **Frank Loesser** wins a Grammy for Best Original Cast Show Album for *"How To Succeed In Business Without Really Trying."*

Maxwell Anderson and **Eugene O'Neill** named among the favorite playwrights in the United States at the New England Theater Conference.

Actor **Fredric March** receives the Stage Diction Medal from the American Academy of Arts and Letters.

Playwright **Clifford Odets** receives the American Academy of Arts and Letters Award of Merit for Drama.

Pulitzer Prize for Drama
All The Way Home
Tad Mosel

French mime **MARCEL MARCEAU** and his company offer a full-scale mime drama based on Gogol's *The Overcoat* in addition to the great mime's solo numbers.

Now You See It, Now You Don't

Julia, Jake And Uncle Joe starring **Claudette Colbert** plays only one night on Broadway making it the fastest closing of a Broadway play in three seasons.

WHAT A YEAR IT WAS!

Art

At The MUSEUM

Kandinsky, Klee, Kokoschka, Grosz, Feininger and **Beckmann** are represented at the Pasadena Art Museum's **German Expressionist** show.

Technology proves several terra-cotta Etruscan figures in the Metropolitan Museum of Art's collection, on display for 40 years, are fake. A confession from the forger backs up the scientific evidence.

Mark Tobey's one-man show at the Louvre features 300 paintings spanning 50 years.

Boston's Museum of Fine Arts and the Los Angeles County Museum mount a comprehensive **Amadeo Modigliani** show.

The Tate Gallery in London now boasts more visitors than the Louvre in Paris.

70 **Henry Moore** sculptures are on view at London's Whitechapel Gallery.

UCLA has a **Picasso** retrospective which includes prints, ceramics, watercolors, drawings and gouaches.

Several self-portraits seen in the U.S. for the first time are among the works lent by the **Van Gogh Foundation** for a one-man show that begins in Baltimore and travels to other American cities.

Says Marcel Duchamp:

"The great artist of tomorrow will go underground."

WHAT A YEAR IT WAS!

At The MUSEUM OF MODERN ART

Matisse's "Le Bateau" hangs upside down for 47 days before the mistake is noticed.

Mark Rothko's retrospective showcases paintings of the last 15 years.

An assemblage exhibit highlights collages and multi-dimensional pieces from the 1880's to the present. Famous names include **Marcel Duchamp, Man Ray, Andre Breton** and **Pablo Picasso**.

The display of **Edward Steichen** photographs spans 65 years.

Max Ernst's first U.S. retrospective features over 200 collages, paintings, drawings and sculpture.

1961

THE NEW YORK ART WORLD

Art meets theatre in a downtown New York exhibition called **"Happenings."** **Claes Oldenburg's** "Ironworks," **Jim Dine's** "Car Crash" and **Robert Whitman's** "The American Moon" are some of the performance pieces that feature artists and their creations.

New Yorkers see their first **Alfred Sisley** exhibit in 40 years.

Alexander Calder mobiles and **Joan Miro** paintings are shown together at a Manhattan gallery.

New York City artists form the Artist Tenants Association to counteract attempts by various city agencies to enforce zoning laws and remove many artists from their low-rent lofts. The association's threat of a boycott of all New York exhibitions helps resolve the situation in favor of loft-dwelling artists throughout the city.

Andy Warhol creates a window display for Manhattan's Lord & Taylor department store using oversized Dick Tracy paintings. He begins painting his Campbell's Soup can series.

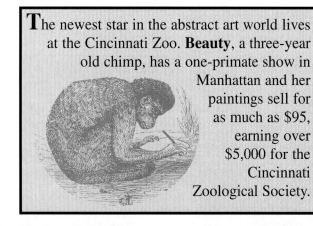

The newest star in the abstract art world lives at the Cincinnati Zoo. **Beauty**, a three-year old chimp, has a one-primate show in Manhattan and her paintings sell for as much as $95, earning over $5,000 for the Cincinnati Zoological Society.

OH, YOKO

Yoko Ono is a new name and her innovative show includes a painting that has a lit candle inserted into it and removed when the painting starts to smoke. Prices range from $75 to $400.

First Lady **Jackie Kennedy** visits the National Gallery to view treasures from King Tutankhamen's tomb.

Jackie begins renovating the White House with art and furnishings from different periods of American history.

New York Governor **Nelson Rockefeller** and his wife **Mary** are forced to flee the Executive Mansion in the middle of the night due to a fire. An estimated 70 pieces of art are ruined or partially damaged, though the Governor saves several Picassos and a drawing by Van Gogh.

A request to Prime Minister **Harold Macmillan** for Britain to return the Elgin Marbles to Greece starts a controversy between the two nations. The marbles have been in the British Museum for 145 years, and popular sentiment among the British seems to lean towards keeping the marbles right where they are.

Sidney Janis Gallery in Manhattan puts on "TEN AMERICANS," featuring contributions by **FRANZ KLINE** ("Contrada"), **ROBERT MOTHERWELL** ("Elegy to the Spanish Republic, 54"), **WILLIAM BAZIOTES** ("Red Landscape"), **MARK ROTHKO** ("Red over Plum and Black") and **WILLEM DE KOONING** ("A Tree in Naples, 1960").

Franz Kline

Robert Motherwell

William Baziotes

WHAT A YEAR IT WAS!

Great Art Can Be A 1961
MOVING Experience

Avant-garde artists put together a collection of modern mobiles on display in Holland that may be art and that certainly move.

This little item not only classifies as far-out sculpture but also turns out dandy abstract paintings.

These young visitors are enjoying their visit to the Municipal Museum of Amsterdam which goes for modern art all the way and should dispose of the old myth about the Dutch being unimaginative.

Whether or not you like the art, it will certainly keep you moving.

1961

PASSINGS

101 years old at the time of her death, primitive painter **GRANDMA MOSES** was in her 70's when the Museum of Modern Art first exhibited her paintings. Grandma's depiction of old-fashioned small-town life gained her fans around the world, and her 100th birthday was declared Grandma Moses Day in New York.

A leader of the Modern art movement, painter and sculptor **MAX WEBER** dies at age 80.

*A **George Grosz** exhibit is one of Chicago's finest art events of the year.*

BARGAIN BASEMENT PRICES

Rembrandt	*"Aristotle Contemplating the Bust of Homer"*	
	$2,300,000 (record price for a painting)	
Monet	*"The Bridge at Argenteuil"*	
	$294,000 (record price for a Monet)	
Picasso	*"Mother and Child"*	
	$532,000 (record price for a living artist)	
Sisley	*"The Inundation"*	**$157,000**
Pollock	*"Free Form—1946"*	**$12,600**

A heretofore unknown Rembrandt self-portrait with a red cap is bought by the Stuttgart Art Gallery for $900,000.

Volkswagen in Wolfsburg, Germany mounts "French Painting from Delacroix to Picasso" featuring canvases by 40 artists loaned from individual collections and museums in 13 countries.

A Milwaukee Jewish Community Center exhibit features works by artists who have lived in Wisconsin, including **Karl Knaths**, **Edward Steichen**, **Georgia O'Keeffe** and **Mark Tobey**.

David Hockney's engravings are on view at the second Biennale de Paris.

Marc Chagall's 12 stained glass windows, each representing 1 of the 12 Tribes of Israel, go on view at a temporary addition to the Louvre. They were created for the synagogue of the Hadassah-Hebrew University Medical Center in Jerusalem.

Henry Moore, Jacques Villon and Rufino Tamayo become Honorary Members of the National Institute of Arts and Letters.

Georgia O'Keeffe

IS THAT A PICASSO IN YOUR POCKET OR ARE YOU JUST HAPPY TO SEE ME?

Thieves have a smashing year, stealing art objects from Pittsburgh to Rome and many cities along the way. Among the pinched names are **Picasso**, **Matisse**, **Utrillo**, **Klee**, **Bonnard**, **Braque**, **Leger**, **Chagall**, **Miro** and **Dufy**.

- - - - - - - - - - - - - - - - -

Stolen from Aix-en-Provence, **Cezanne's** "The Card Players" is worth $1 million.

- - - - - - - - - - - - - - - - -

Goya's "Portrait of the Duke of Wellington," just sold for $392,000, is pilfered from the National Gallery in London.

- - - - - - - - - - - - - - - - -

The 57 paintings taken from the Annonciade Museum in St. Tropez are valued at approximately $2 million.

Pittsburgh International Exhibition at the CARNEGIE INSTITUTE

1st Prize, painting **Mark Tobey**

1st Prize, sculpture **Alberto Giacometti**

WHAT A YEAR IT WAS!

ARCHITECTURE
+ DESIGN

Urbanist **Lewis Mumford** worries *"that every city is becoming a parking lot city."*

•

Architect **Edward Durrell Stone** believes bad planning has contributed to turning the United States from *"the most beautiful country on earth to the ugliest"* and considers Los Angeles the most hideous American metropolis.

Chase Manhattan Bank

moves into its new headquarters at One Chase Manhattan Plaza, New York. Designed by Skidmore, Owings & Merrill, the 60-story aluminum and glass building also has, at Chase Manhattan President David Rockefeller's insistence, lots of trees on the street-level plaza. Original artwork worth $1/2 million decorates executive offices and common areas.

Milan's 12th Triennale features a special exhibit of **Frank Lloyd Wright's** *work.*

Nearly **$58 billion** is spent on new construction.

Construction continues on the $100 million Pan Am Building in Manhattan with an estimated December, 1962 completion date.

An idea is floated to build a small island for habitation on Manhattan's East River to ease the burgeoning growth of the city.

Plans are submitted to the Santa Monica, California Redevelopment Agency for a skyscraper city that will include apartments, an office building, a motel, stores and gardens near the beach in the Ocean Park section of town.

Some of 20th Century Fox Studios' sets are destroyed to make way for Century City.

Ground is broken in **St. Louis, Missouri** for **Eero Saarinen's Gateway Arch**.

WHAT A YEAR IT WAS!

135

1961

Mies van der Rohe:

- is at work on his first European edifice in decades, an administration building for Krupp Industries in Essen, Germany.

- is elected to the National Institute of Arts and Letters.

The kitchen pantry makes a comeback.

Trompe-l'oeil is a popular decorating tool, used mainly for wallpaper.

Le Corbusier

The American Institute of Architects bestows Le Corbusier with its Gold Medal. Says the great architect, *"I only believe what I have seen, and to see everything in architecture is a dog's life."*

Construction begins on Le Corbusier's Visual Arts Center at Harvard, his first structure in the United States.

Le Corbusier receives an award from the Franklin Institute for "startling concepts of modern architecture and city planning."

GOOD FOR THE TUSH

SWIVEL CHAIRS make office life easier.

EERO SAARINEN designs pedestal chairs with cushy foam interiors and, for the first time, a completely upholstered exterior.

WHEN PRESIDENT KENNEDY gets a rocking chair he unwittingly starts a national craze and some furniture manufacturers have trouble keeping up with the demand.

CHARLES EAMES creates a new plastic shell chair with aluminum legs for restaurant use.

The National Institute of Arts and Letters gives I.M. Pei its Brunner Award.

The average price of a house nationwide is roughly $14,000.

Approximately 250,000 swimming pools are built in California backyards.

PASSINGS

Finnish-born architect **Eero Saarinen**, member of the American Academy of Arts and Letters, designed buildings for TWA, IBM, MIT, General Motors, American embassies in Oslo and London and the terminal at Dulles International Airport. Saarinen, who won the competition for the Jefferson National Expansion Memorial in St. Louis, Missouri with his stainless steel arch design, dies at age 51 following surgery for a brain tumor.

WHAT A YEAR IT WAS!

This is New Woodhue—solid vinyl tile with the rich look and _feel_ of fine parquet flooring!

FLOOR: WOODHUE VINYL TILES V950, V951
COSTUME: BONNIE CASHIN

The key to the smart woman's styling secret: coordination
Congoleum-Nairn **Vinyl** Floors

Imagine the beauty of this deep-grained Woodhue vinyl tile in your home! So easy to coordinate with furnishings. So like expensive wood parquet. You can actually feel the deep graining in new Woodhue by Congoleum-Nairn. Yet, in most 12' x 15' rooms, this lovely solid vinyl floor costs about $85—installed!

Send for free sample of new Woodhue (just ONE of our 405 masterpieces), and Decor-Key Kit filled with exciting new decorating ideas. Write Congoleum-Nairn, 200 Belgrove Dr., Kearny, N. J.

Congoleum-Nairn
FINE FLOORS

137

Books

A Burnt-Out Case
Graham Greene

A Journey To Matecumbe
Robert Lewis Taylor

A Nation Of Sheep
William Lederer

A New Life
Bernard Malamud

A Severed Head
Iris Murdoch

A Shooting Star
Wallace Stegner

Adrift In Soho
Colin Wilson

The Age Of Reason Begins
Will Durant

The Agony And The Ecstasy
Irving Stone

The American Express
Gregory Corso

**The American Theatre As Seen
By Hirshfeld**
Al Hirshfeld

An American Visitor
Joyce Cary

**The Autobiography of
Eleanor Roosevelt**

Bayonets To Lhasa
Peter Fleming

Book Of Dreams
Jack Kerouac

Boy, Girl. Boy, Girl.
Jules Feiffer

Calories Don't Count
Dr. Herman Taller

The Carpetbaggers
Harold Robbins

Catch-22
Joseph Heller

The City In History
Lewis Mumford

Clock Without Hands
Carson McCullers

The Cloud Forest
Peter Mathiessen

Daughter Of Silence
Morris West

Dawn
Elie Wiesel

The Deep
Mickey Spillane

Don't Tell Alfred
Nancy Mitford

Dr. Spock Talks With Mothers
Dr. Benjamin Spock

The Drug Experience
David Ebin

The Edge Of Sadness
Edwin O'Connor

Eight Men
Richard Wright

False Entry
Hortense Calisher

Foods For Glamour
Jack LaLanne

For The New Intellectual
Ayn Rand

Fourteen Stories
Pearl S. Buck

Franny And Zooey
J.D. Salinger

God Must Be Sad
Fannie Hurst

Harpo Speaks!
Harpo Marx

Heaven Has No Favorites
Erich Maria Remarque

How Much Is That In Dollars?
Art Buchwald

**How To Keep Slender And Fit
After Thirty**
Bonnie Prudden

PRIZES

NOBEL

Literature
IVO ANDRIC, YUGOSLAVIA

PULITZER

Public Service
Amarillo (Texas) Globe-Times

National Reporting
EDWARD R. CONY
The Wall Street Journal

International Reporting
LYNN HEINZERLING, *AP*

Editorial Cartooning
CAREY ORR, *Chicago Tribune*

Photography
YASUSHI NAGAO, *Mainichi*

Fiction
HARPER LEE
"To Kill A Mockingbird"

History
HERBERT FEIS
*"Between War And Peace:
The Potsdam Conference"*

Biography or Autobiography
DAVID DONALD
*"Charles Sumner And The
Coming Of The Civil War"*

Poetry
PHYLLIS McGINLEY
*"Times Three: Selected Verse
From
Three
Decades"*

I Should Have Kissed Her More
Alexander King

In Place Of Folly
Norman Cousins

In The Arms Of The Mountain
Elizabeth Seeman

Inside Europe Today
John Gunther

Lanterns And Lances
James Thurber

Life With Women And
How To Survive It
Joseph H. Peck

Living Free
Joy Adamson

The Magic Of Their Singing
Bernard Wolfe

The Making Of The President, 1960
Theodore H. White

The Man-Eater Of Malgudi
R.K. Narayan

Marx's Concept Of Man
Erich Fromm

Men And Women
Erskine Caldwell

Midcentury
John Dos Passos

Mila 18
Leon Uris

The Morning And The Evening
Joan Williams

Mothers And Daughters
Evan Hunter

The Moviegoer
Walker Percy

My Place In The Bazaar
Alex Waugh

My Saber Is Bent
Jack Paar & John Reddy

The New Book, A Book
Of Torture
Michael McClure

New York:
A Serendipiter's Journey
Gay Talese

No Mother To Guide Her
Anita Loos

Nobody Knows My Name
James Baldwin

The Old Men At The Zoo
Angus Wilson

On The Contrary
Mary McCarthy

The Prime Of Miss Jean Brodie
Muriel Spark

PT109, John F. Kennedy In
World War II
Robert Donovan

Sketches From Life Of Men
I Have Known
Dean Acheson

The Soft Machine
William S. Burroughs

Some People, Places And Things
That Will Not Appear In My
Next Novel
John Cheever

The Spinoza Of Market Street
Isaac Bashevis Singer

Spirit Lake
MacKinlay Kantor

Starting From San Francisco
Lawrence Ferlinghetti

The Story Of A Novel
Thomas Mann

Stranger In A Strange Land
Robert A. Heinlein

Thunderball
Ian Fleming

The Twenty-Seventh Wife
Irving Wallace

The White Rajah
Nicholas Monsarrat

Wilderness
Robert Penn Warren

The Winter Of Our Discontent
John Steinbeck

Passings

Often thought of as the greatest 20th Century American author, Nobel Prize winner **Ernest Hemingway** dies at age 61 of a self-inflicted gunshot wound to the head. Bullfight aficionado, member of the lost generation, one-time expatriate writer in Paris and overall larger-than-life character, Hemingway's contribution to literature includes the Pulitzer Prize winning *"The Old Man and the Sea," "For Whom the Bell Tolls," "The Sun Also Rises"* and *"A Farewell to Arms."*

Dashiell Hammett, best known for his detective character Sam Spade and his novels *"The Maltese Falcon"* and *"The Thin Man,"* dies at age 66. Former Pinkerton private eye, Hammett once spent six months in jail for refusing to name contributors to a Communist organization's bail fund.

James Thurber — playwright, essayist, cartoonist, author, humorist, creator of Walter Mitty, early staff member of THE NEW YORKER and former newspaper reporter — dies at age 66. A code clerk in Paris during World War I, Thurber kept drawing and writing even after losing his eyesight.

139

1961

Books

"To Sir, With Love" earns **E.R. Braithwaite** the Anisfield-Wolf Award, given for books with the topic of race relations, along with "The Reluctant African" by **Louis Lomax**.

Grace Paley receives a Guggenheim Fellowship.

Winston Churchill, E.M. Forster and **Somerset Maugham** among the authors named the first Companions of Literature by The Royal Society of Literature.

Thomas Pynchon wins an O. Henry Prize for his short story "Under the Rose."

"The Rise and Fall of the Third Reich" wins **William L. Shirer** a National Book Award and an Overseas Press Club Award.

Jack Kerouac writes *"Big Sur."*

Marlene Dietrich

works on her first book, *"Marlene Dietrich's ABC."*

Robert Frost

recites *"The Gift Outright"* at President Kennedy's inauguration and becomes Poet Laureate of Vermont.

Best-Selling Book Of The Year
"The New English Bible: New Testament."

Dietrich

Computer technology helps Columbia University student **James McDonough** solve the age-old question of whether the **"Iliad"** was written by one person. He determines that **Homer** is indeed the sole author.

A first edition of Miguel de Cervantes' *"Don Quixote"* sells at auction for $44,000.

Cervantes

Norman Mailer gives a reading in New York and after reciting some poetry with less-than-gentlemanly language is forced off the stage.

- - - - - - - - - - -

An unexpurgated version of **Henry Miller's** "Tropic of Cancer" is finally available in the United States. The Post Office refuses to deliver the book.

Visited by thousands of people a day, the New York Public Library turns 50.

The American Library Association amends its Bill of Rights —
"The rights of an individual to the use of the library should not be denied or abridged because of his race, religion, national origins or political views."

Professor **John Kemeny** envisions the library for the year 2000 will have 10 million volumes and books stored on tape. Also, users will be able to phone into libraries and get necessary information on individual viewing screens.

WHAT A YEAR IT WAS!

DISASTERS

1961

Powerful hurricane Carla hits the Texas and Louisiana coasts causing floods and tornadoes as far away as Missouri and Kansas. The weather satellite Tiros III helps meteorologists track the storm, which in turn helps 1/2 million people flee the Texas coast before Carla hits. Over 30 die and damage is estimated at $1 billion.

- Heavy snowfall kills 100 within two days on the East Coast.

- 163 counties in the Great Plains are hit by a drought and declared disaster areas. Saskatchewan, Alberta and Manitoba Canada also suffer.

- A mud slide kills 145 in Kiev, USSR.

- In Bihar, India floods take the lives of 700 people, including 100 youngsters.

- Hurricane Tara takes the lives of 430 people in Guerrero State, Mexico.

9 firemen are killed when a wall collapses in a Chicago fire.

Over 300 people die and 800 are hurt when a circus fire is set by a former employee in Niteroi, Brazil.

A fire aboard "Dara" in the Persian Gulf kills 212.

A fire in California's Sierra Mountains destroys nearly 19,000 acres.

A coal mine fire in Fukuoka, Japan kills 71 miners.

In Dolna Suce, Czechoslovakia a coal mine gas explosion kills 108.

1961

43 Moroccan Jews, on their way to Israel via Gibraltar, drown in a boat off the coast of Spanish Morocco.

23 Burmese drown when a truck returning from a Buddhist celebration falls into a stream.

Automobile deaths over the 4th of July holiday weekend reach an all-time high of 509.

70 die in Catanzaro, Italy when the last car of a train disengages and crashes into a ravine.

———

A train hits a school bus near Greeley, Colorado, killing 20 children.

- A French Air Force jet accidentally cuts a cable sending several cable cars in the French Alps to the snowy ground hundreds of feet below. Six die instantly and 81 must wait for help.

- At the Tibet-India border 62 people die when a bridge under construction gives way.

- A bus crashes into a canyon in Prijepolje, Yugoslavia, killing 39.

AIRLINE CRASH DEATHS

- - - - - - - -

Santiago, Chile: 28

Seville, Spain: 30

Prades, France: 34

Stavanger, Norway: 39

Ruesselback, West Germany: 52

Lisbon, Portugal: 62

Azul, Argentina: 67

Casablanca, Morocco: 72

Brussels, Belgium: 73

Richmond, Virginia: 77

Edjele, Algeria: 79

Shannon, Ireland: 84

- - - - - - - -

The worst commercial plane crash in U.S. history occurs near Chicago's Midway Airport, killing all 78 people aboard. The airliner was traveling from the East Coast to the West Coast.

FASHION

Its All About *Jackie*

More important than Dior, Cardin or Balanciaga, America's First Lady is the world's first lady of fashion. Designers and women everywhere follow Jackie's lead.

For her husband's inauguration, Jackie wears a long white chiffon gown topped by an embroidered silver camisole and long gloves.

Oleg Cassini continues to create most of her wardrobe.

On Easter, Jackie goes to church in a silk dress and straw pillbox hat, but on Good Friday she is more casual in sandals sans hosiery.

The **"Jackie Look"** includes pillbox hats, slim suits, sleeveless and collarless dresses, a less-is-more approach, understated elegance, pearls and long skirts.

Jackie is voted the best-dressed woman in the world for the second year in a row. Sister Princess Radziwill makes the list for the first time.

Jackie causes a minor scandal when she buys a dress made by Paris designer *Givenchy.*

WHAT A YEAR IT WAS!

1961

If It's *New Hat Time*

Winter's chill may be less stinging with the unveiling of a new collection of hats for the new season.

This one is trimmed with two large roses, very feminine and just right for the coming season.

Here's a perky chapeau of Italian straw.

Here's a convertible eye-catching white toque (left) with an on-again off-again straw picture brim (right).

144

Can *Spring* Be Far Away?

Black leather has interesting possibilities too.

Dark satin, trimmed in black, gives this creation after-dark flattery.

To enhance a mood, add a horsehair veil to this straw toque.

Sou'westers are in, to make sure this season won't pass without its fashion controversy. Call it chic or call it a coal scuttle, as you will. You have to admit, it's striking.

COLORS & FABRICS

polka dots, grey, corduroy, pink, flannel, turquoise, Irish linen, yellow, chiffon, orange, felt, brown, paisley, lilac, fleece, red, velvet, blue, worsted, green, silk, copper, crepe, white, velour, black, damask, purple, tweed

- jersey
- culottes

Dresses

- sashes
- fringe
- one-shoulder
- princess styling
- narrow or flared
- bias cut

1961

Suits

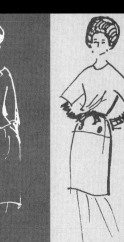

"The Look"

- shorter
- slimmer skirts ending at the knee
- loose-fitting jackets just hitting the hips
- large buttons
- wider shoulders

Thigh-high skirt slits cause a furor in Hong Kong, while on the mainland the government forces women to wear their skirts ankle-length.

•

Prints are popular on suits, dresses, sweaters and blouses.

1961

all in a day

Day

sleeveless & collarless tops and dresses, large straw hats, gloves with matching shoes, flared skirts, cape coats, loose-fitting blouses

Leisure

bell-bottoms, wide belts, sandals

Evening

glamorous short or long dresses, slender, sleeveless, fitted bodices, beads, brocade, lame, satin, taffeta, lace, long gloves

The costly "little nothing" dress is a staple.

Jewels

Most jewels have gilt, fringe, faux stones or beads.

Options include:

- Real or fake pearls and gold
  - Giant pendants
  - Two matching bracelets worn together
- Large drop earrings
- Multi-strand necklaces
  - Rhinestone pins
  - Huge rings

If it's big and bright, it's all right.

A RAOUL DUFY print decorates a dress from JAMES GALANOS.

Hip huggers are all the rage with California designers, usually topped with a short blouse, allowing the wearers' midsections to be seen by all. Though not a new style, the designers are hoping it finally catches on with American women. So far only in the South of France, where drop waist pants are tight around the ankles and topped by midriff-baring bolero tops, are women willing to expose all.

See-through bathing suits, clear in all but the most private spots, are new.

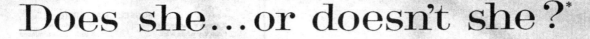

Does she...or doesn't she?*

Hair color so natural only her hairdresser knows for sure!

That wonderful feeling of security, so precious at any age, thrives on approval. *This* is as true for mothers as it is for babies—and she knows it! Her warmth, her fresh good looks, the radiant color of her hair reflect it! And when you think how quick and easy it is to keep hair beautiful with Miss Clairol, you wonder why *any* woman *ever* should let gray or fading color age her looks or undermine her confidence.

Hairdressers everywhere prefer Miss Clairol to all other haircolorings and recommend it as the haircoloring that truly lives up to its promise. Its automatic color timing is most dependable. And Miss Clairol *really* covers gray. But best of all, it keeps hair silky, lovely, completely natural-looking! So try Miss Clairol yourself. Today. Comes in Creme Formula or Regular.

Guaranteed by
Good Housekeeping

MISS CLAIROL* HAIR COLOR BATH†
THE NATURAL-LOOKING HAIRCOLORING • MORE WOMEN USE MISS CLAIROL THAN ALL OTHER HAIRCOLORING COMBINED
*Reg'd Trademarks, †HAIR COLOR BATH is a trademark of Clairol Incorporated. Also available in Canada.   ©1961 Clairol Incorporated, Stamford, Conn.

150

a shoe-in

dainty, high, slim, pointy-toed heels remain standard for formal evenings.

Square toes with low or medium, squat or thin heels with decorative bows are worn all hours of the day or night. The new look in toes is created by **Roger Vivier**, shoe designer for the **House of Dior**.

Canvas sneakers are for casual fun.

most American ladies buy a minimum of five pair of shoes a year.

multi-colored and patterned shoes for anytime.

for girls, bottle caps decorate their school shoes.

1961

I LIKE A HAT LIKE THAT

Enormous or petit, hat styles include the breton, calot, dome, beret, sailor, straw sombrero, skull cap and saucer.

Decorations include flowers and ribbons.

THE HAT OF THE YEAR IS THE PILLBOX, MADE STYLISH BY JACKIE.

Perennially well-dressed actress *Audrey Hepburn* is voted into the Fashion Hall of Fame.

The Duchess of Windsor, continually on the world's best-dressed lists, surprises the fashion world when she buys American designs while visiting Manhattan.

WHAT A YEAR IT WAS!

The Latest From Paris

Givenchy offers beading, embroidery and sleeveless coats for evening.

COCO CHANEL PRESENTS SLIM SUITS WITH SLENDER SKIRTS AND SINGLE OR DOUBLE-BREASTED JACKETS, PINK SUITS AND PINK BLOUSES, GOLD BUTTONS, POCKETS WITH BUTTONS AND PLEATED DRESSES.

HOODS

ON SUITS, BLOUSES AND COATS ARE SEEN AT SEVERAL FASHION SHOWS.

Andre Courreges presents his first fashion collection.

Marc Bohan has his first showing as head of the House of Dior, which includes dresses with lower waistlines and shorter hemlines. Bohan is the chief proponent of the flapper look, which is worn on both sides of the Atlantic.

1961

Short hair
with bangs,
a side part
and a few
curls at the cheeks is a perfect look
for almost anyone.
Layers give added height.

*hair,
there and
everywhere*

Little 4-year old AISSA WAYNE, daughter
of JOHN WAYNE, is the latest cover girl,
seen on COSMOPOLITAN's 75th anniversary
issue. Aissa is bedecked in over $800,000
of diamonds from Cartier's.

BEVERLY VALDES becomes the
first high-fashion, full-time
black staff model in America.

MR. KENNETH, who created
Jackie's bouffant hairdo and also coifs
Marilyn Monroe and Judy Garland,
wins a Coty American Fashion Critics'
Award, the first time the award has gone
to a hairstylist. The bouffant is the most
copied look of the year.

Wigs match the colors of cars.

make-up and more

Pastel colored lipstick, colorful blue, green or violet eye shadow under thick eyebrows and pink rouge make the perfect face.

COVER GIRL make-up is introduced.

THE HOUSE OF REVLON opens on Manhattan's Fifth Avenue, offering Roman decor, $10 massages and $5 manicures.

NARROW TIES ARE ALL THE RAGE.

MEN

WAISTCOATS BECOME PREVALENT FOR THE FIRST TIME SINCE THE 1940'S.

PRESIDENT KENNEDY'S PENCHANT FOR TWO-BUTTON SUITS INSTEAD OF THE POPULAR THREE STARTS A TREND AMONG AMERICAN MEN.

FASHION MOVES FORWARD IN RELIGIOUS CIRCLES TOO AS PRIESTS IN MONTREAL ARE TOLD TO STOP WEARING THEIR CENTURIES-OLD CASSOCK UNIFORMS AND BEGIN WEARING BLACK SUITS.

WHAT A YEAR IT WAS!

1961

*F*ashions for men tailored by some of the Continent's leading stylists take the spotlight for summer starting with this belted jacket and fancy vest.

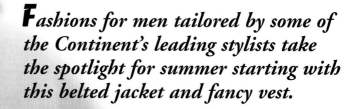

FAR-OUT
Fashions For Men

*I*t's a turnabout from the usual fashion show in which the usually drab male sets off the colorful attire of the opposite sex.

*T*he American influence is apparent in this cocktail cowboy suit (left) with Fancy Dan cuffs on the trousers. (below)

*P*lenty of fancy trim is evident on this suit.

*T*his well-dressed couple is ready for a night on the town.

1961

IN ADDITION TO BEING THE MOST TALENTED MAN IN SHOW BUSINESS, SINGER-ACTOR-ACADEMY AWARD WINNER FRANK SINATRA IS ONE OF THE BEST DRESSED, AND PURCHASES A NEW WARDROBE FOR A CRUISE WITH HIS FAMOUS CLAN. ITEMS INCLUDE CASUAL AND FORMAL WEAR MADE BY SY DEVORE, CLOTHIER TO THE STARS.

HOLLYWOOD DESIGNER DON LOPER DESIGNS FRANK SINATRA'S WARDROBE FOR PRESIDENT KENNEDY'S INAUGURATION.

WHAT A YEAR IT WAS!

Look smarter, feel better...

ENJOY JARMAN'S FAMOUS FRIENDLINESS OF FIT!

"Snug-A-Matic" Styles

Here is a new concept in slip-on shoes: leather-covered elastic gives sure, snug fit and eliminates for all time that worrisome slipping and sliding. No laces to tie; just slip them on and go — they're "Snug-A-Matic!" Available at your Jarman dealer's. (Each style shown here also comes in black.)

Jarman shoes available at Jarman dealers and Jarman stores, $10.95 to $19.95 most styles. Jarman Jrs. for boys, $8.95 and $9.95 most styles.

JARMAN SHOE COMPANY • NASHVILLE, TENNESSEE A Genesco Division

Jarman
SHOES FOR MEN

158

SPORTS 1961

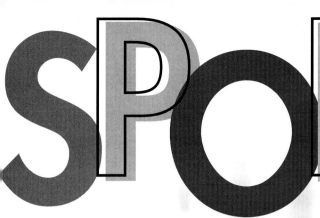

ROGER MARIS
BREAKS THE BABE'S HOME RUN RECORD

New York Yankee Roger Maris leads the assault to break Babe Ruth's 60 home run record set in 1927.

It isn't until the final game of the season that it happens. Maris waits for the pitch (*right*) swings and hits the ball into the stands (*background photo*) for his 61st home run, making the 27-year old the first Major League player to hit more than 60 home runs in a season.

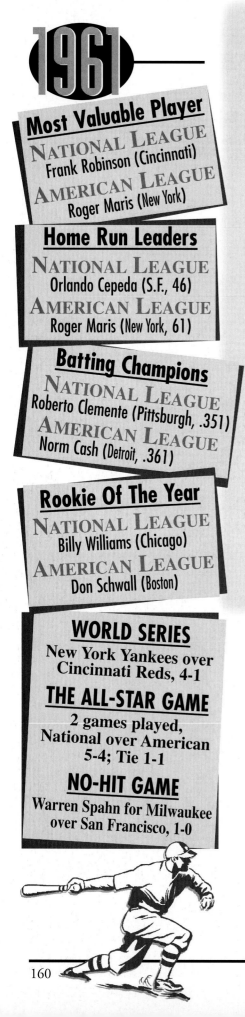

Most Valuable Player

NATIONAL LEAGUE
Frank Robinson (Cincinnati)
AMERICAN LEAGUE
Roger Maris (New York)

Home Run Leaders

NATIONAL LEAGUE
Orlando Cepeda (S.F., 46)
AMERICAN LEAGUE
Roger Maris (New York, 61)

Batting Champions

NATIONAL LEAGUE
Roberto Clemente (Pittsburgh, .351)
AMERICAN LEAGUE
Norm Cash (Detroit, .361)

Rookie Of The Year

NATIONAL LEAGUE
Billy Williams (Chicago)
AMERICAN LEAGUE
Don Schwall (Boston)

WORLD SERIES

New York Yankees over
Cincinnati Reds, 4-1

THE ALL-STAR GAME

2 games played,
National over American
5-4; Tie 1-1

NO-HIT GAME

Warren Spahn for Milwaukee
over San Francisco, 1-0

BASEBALL NEWS

Leo Durocher signs on as a coach for the Los Angeles DODGERS.

New York Yankee **MICKEY MANTLE** (29) signs a $75,000 contract, a $10,000 raise over last year.

In a game against the Minnesota Twins, Baltimore Oriole **JIM GENTILE** sets a Major League record by hitting two grand-slam home runs in two consecutive innings.

Hall of Famer
JOE DiMAGGIO
comes out of retirement for two weeks to serve as a special assistant to new Yankees manager Ralph Houk.

Former New York Yankees manager **CASEY STENGEL** returns to baseball to manage the New York Mets.

After Governor Rockefeller signs a bill permitting New York to build an $18 million 55,000-seat baseball stadium, **ground is broken in Flushing Meadows for SHEA STADIUM**, the future home of the New York Mets.

With the addition of two new franchises in Minnesota and Los Angeles, for the first time since its inauguration in 1901 the American League has ten teams instead of eight.

WHAT A YEAR IT WAS!

YANKEES
In The World Series Again!

1961

Fans pack the stadium to watch the Yankees play against the Cincinnati Reds.

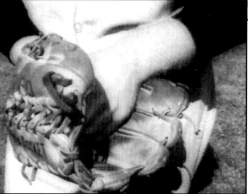

Whitey Ford leads the assault and pitches brilliant ball.

His pitching along with the power of Yankee sluggers Maris and Mantle gives them the World Championship, four games to one with Ford completing 32 consecutive scoreless innings.

WHAT A YEAR IT WAS!

Nothing shaves like a blade –

that's why Sunbeam put 3 real blades in the new Shavemaster to shave closer, get beard other razors can't get

1. *Bradley University, 8:25 P.M.: interviewer stops student Jack Sulka and date on their way to the DU Sweetheart Ball.*

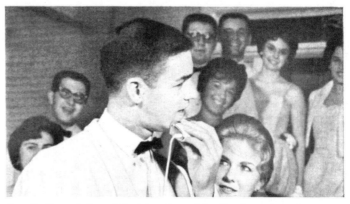

2. *Sulka points out that he shaved for the formal one hour ago, but agrees to try again with a Shavemaster shaver.*

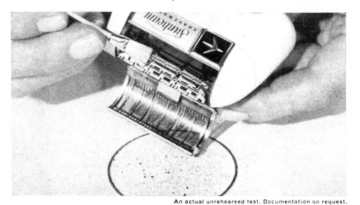

An actual unrehearsed test. Documentation on request.

3. *Interviewer flips shaver head open and brushes beard onto paper...beard Sulka's own razor missed!*

4. *Seeing proof of the closer Shavemaster shave, Sulka says, "No date complaints now! This shave is a whole lot closer!"*

THIS actual, unrehearsed test proves that the new Sunbeam Shavemaster shaver gives you a closer, more comfortable shave than any electric ever could before. This new Sunbeam introduces a basic new design. It shaves you with real blades.

Three real blades—locked inside its rounded head —give you a shave so close, it has to be compared with the results you get from a straight razor or the sharpest safety blade. No matter how you hold it, you don't feel the slightest pull or irritation. For your convenience, it has a long hair trimmer, flip-open shaving head and on-off switch.

A handsome presentation case makes the Sunbeam Shavemaster perfect for Father's Day and graduation giving! See it at dealers now.

Ask for the shaver with the 3 real blades

Great gift from Dad to Grad (and vice versa)

NEW Sunbeam SHAVEMASTER
ELECTRIC SHAVER

162

Suggested retail price, $32.50   Sunbeam Corporation, Chicago 50, Ill., Canada: Toronto 18 ®Sunbeam Shavemaster

GIANTS BEAT THE BRAVES 14-4 IN MILWAUKEE AND WILLIE MAYS MAKES BASEBALL HISTORY

1961

Hitless in this series until today, Willie Mays smashes his first of four home runs in a single game.

Willie thought he was in a batting slump but bounces back with a vengeance scattering baseballs into the bleachers and almost single-handedly leads the Giants to their win.

Only eight men including the great Lou Gehrig have hit four home runs in one game and today Willie becomes the ninth, joining that select circle.

It's Mays day in Milwaukee as Willie finds his page in the record book.

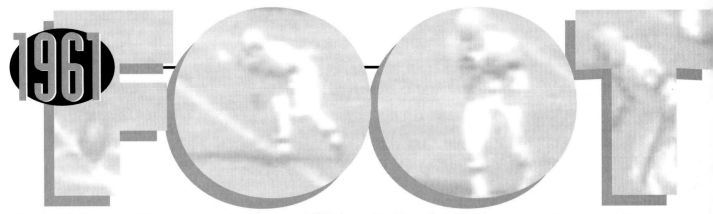

1961 FOOT

Football provides some spine-chilling thrills in the season's pro opener

TIM BROWN of the Philadelphia Eagles takes the opening kick-off from five yards behind his goal line and romps 105 yards for a touchdown.

Syracuse's Ernie Davis (#44) is the Heisman Trophy winner as the outstanding college football player of the year.

Ohio State has a brilliant season and one of the reasons is Chuck Bryant, who takes a pass and snakes his way for a 62-yard tally.

Dave Ramey of Michigan takes an Ohio State kick-off all the way home.

WHAT A YEAR IT WAS!

BALL

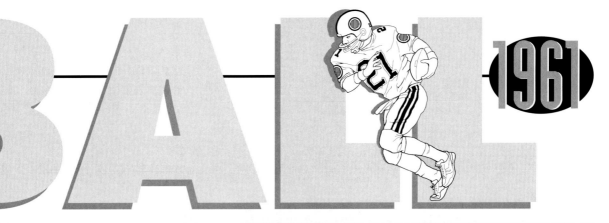

1961

NATIONAL FOOTBALL LEAGUE CHAMPIONS

Green Bay Packers
over **New York Giants**, 37-0*

*Green Bay running back PAUL HORNUNG is called up by the U.S. Army Reserve in the middle of the season but is allowed to leave camp every Sunday so that he can carry and kick the ball for his team.

AMERICAN FOOTBALL LEAGUE CHAMPIONS

Houston Oilers
over **San Diego Chargers**, 10-3

NFL ROOKIE OF THE YEAR

MIKE DITKA, **Chicago**

NFL MOST VALUABLE PLAYER

PAUL HORNUNG, **Green Bay Packers**

NFL NUMBER ONE DRAFT CHOICE

TOMMY MASON,
halfback, **Tulane** to **Minnesota**

AMERICAN FOOTBALL COACHES ASSOCIATION COACH OF THE YEAR

BEAR BRYANT, **Alabama**

HEISMAN TROPHY

ERNIE DAVIS, **Syracuse**, Halfback*
*First black to win

NATIONAL COLLEGE FOOTBALL CHAMPIONS

Alabama & Ohio State

FOOTBALL NOTES

VINCE LOMBARDI is coach of the Green Bay Packers.

L.A. Chargers move to San Diego.

31-YEAR OLD New York Giants halfback **Frank Gifford** announces his retirement to become a sports broadcaster with WCBS Radio in New York.

IN A SURPRISE VICTORY led by rookie quarterback **Fran Tarkenton,** the Minnesota Vikings expansion team defeat the veteran Chicago Bears 37-13 in their first NFL game.

BUD WILKINSON, head football coach at the University of Oklahoma, is called to Washington by President Kennedy to become special consultant to the President's Council on Youth Fitness.

NFL PRO BOWL

West over
East, 35-31

ROSE BOWL

Washington
over
Minnesota,
17-7

1961 BASKETBALL

A capacity crowd of 14,000 packs the stands to watch the NBA finals between the Boston Celtics and the St. Louis Hawks.

Bill Russell, #6, brilliantly spearheads the Celtics.

The St. Louis Hawks fight back to trail by only five points in the third period.

Then, Cousy and company start clicking.

The Boston quintet dazzles the St. Louis Hawks with their fast break attack.

The fans go wild!

WHAT A YEAR IT WAS!

in Boston

Playmaker Cousy, #14, is in evidence all through the play-offs.

With time running out, the Celtics have a solid lead but they're still going.

They clinch the series, four games to one with a winning score of 121 to 112.

Cousy stops exhausted as the final buzzer sounds.

The Celtics win their third straight title.

1961

NBA CHAMPIONS
Boston Celtics over St. Louis Hawks, 4-1

NBA Scoring Leader (Season)
Wilt Chamberlain, 3,033 points*

*first NBA player to accumulate more than 3,000 points in a single season

NBA Scoring Leader (Single Game)
Wilt Chamberlain, 78–record

NBA REBOUNDS (Season)
Wilt Chamberlain, Philadelphia, 2,149–record

NBA FIELD GOAL PERCENTAGE (Season)
Wilt Chamberlain, .509–record

NBA FIELD GOALS (Single Game)
Wilt Chamberlain, 31–record

MOST VALUABLE PLAYER
Bill Russell, Boston Celtics

ROOKIE of the YEAR
Oscar Robertson, Cincinnati

NBA All-Star Game
West over East, 153-131

NCAA CHAMPIONS
Cincinnati over Ohio State, 70-65

NCAA MOST OUTSTANDING PLAYER
Jerry Lucas, Ohio State

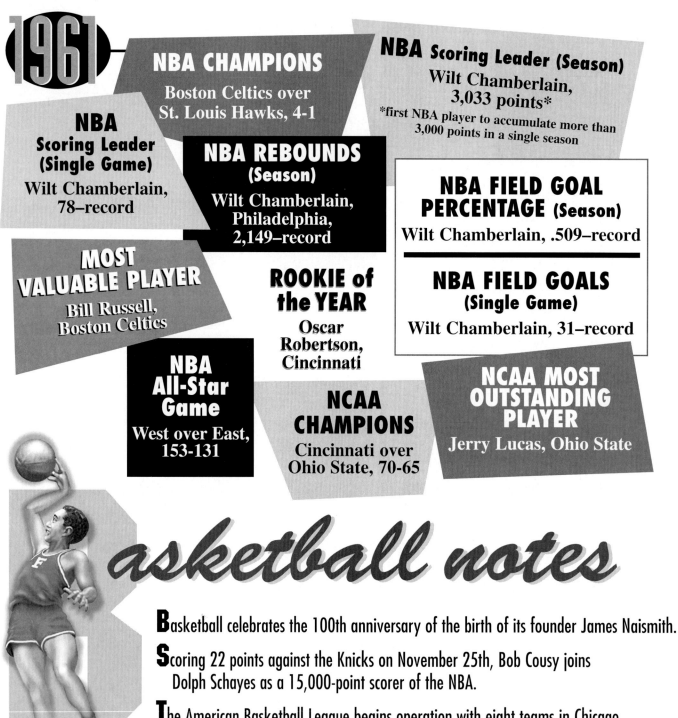

Basketball notes

Basketball celebrates the 100th anniversary of the birth of its founder James Naismith.

Scoring 22 points against the Knicks on November 25th, Bob Cousy joins Dolph Schayes as a 15,000-point scorer of the NBA.

The American Basketball League begins operation with eight teams in Chicago, Cleveland, Honolulu, Kansas City, Los Angeles, Pittsburgh, San Francisco and Washington.

Chicago joins the NBA bringing the total number of teams to nine.

Construction begins for the Basketball Hall of Fame in Springfield, Massachusetts.

39 players from 22 colleges including Columbia, Detroit, Mississippi State, Oregon, North Carolina and Philadelphia's St. Joseph are implicated in the second betting scandal in a decade to rock college basketball.

WHAT A YEAR IT WAS!

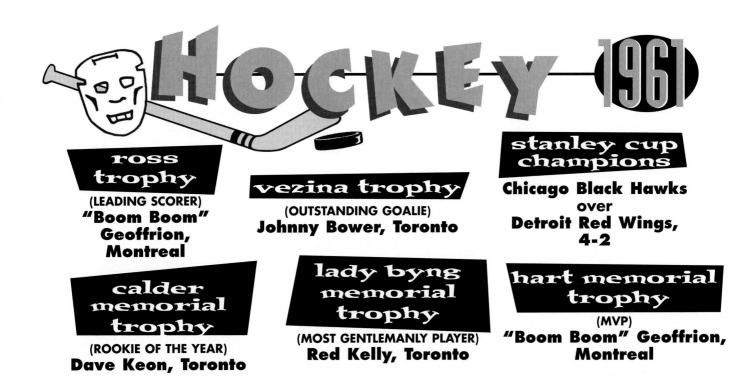

HOCKEY 1961

ross trophy
(LEADING SCORER)
"Boom Boom" Geoffrion, Montreal

vezina trophy
(OUTSTANDING GOALIE)
Johnny Bower, Toronto

stanley cup champions
Chicago Black Hawks over Detroit Red Wings, 4-2

calder memorial trophy
(ROOKIE OF THE YEAR)
Dave Keon, Toronto

lady byng memorial trophy
(MOST GENTLEMANLY PLAYER)
Red Kelly, Toronto

hart memorial trophy
(MVP)
"Boom Boom" Geoffrion, Montreal

the hockey hall of fame
opens at the Canadian National Exhibition in Toronto.

horse racing

KENTUCKY DERBY
Carry Back,
ridden by Johnny Sellers

PREAKNESS
Carry Back,
ridden by Johnny Sellers

BELMONT STAKES
Sherluck,
ridden by Braulio Baeza

HORSE OF THE YEAR
Kelso

MONEY LEADERS
JOCKEY
Willie Shoemaker, $2,690,819
HORSE
Carry Back, $565,349

NOTES

 Crimson Satan takes Garden State Stakes in the world's richest horse race.

 Willie Shoemaker aboard **Guaranteeya** wins the 4,000th race of his career at Hollywood Park on May 19th.

 The Argentine team wins Nations Cup in National Horse Show in New York.

OK

WHAT A YEAR IT WAS!

OK

OK

169

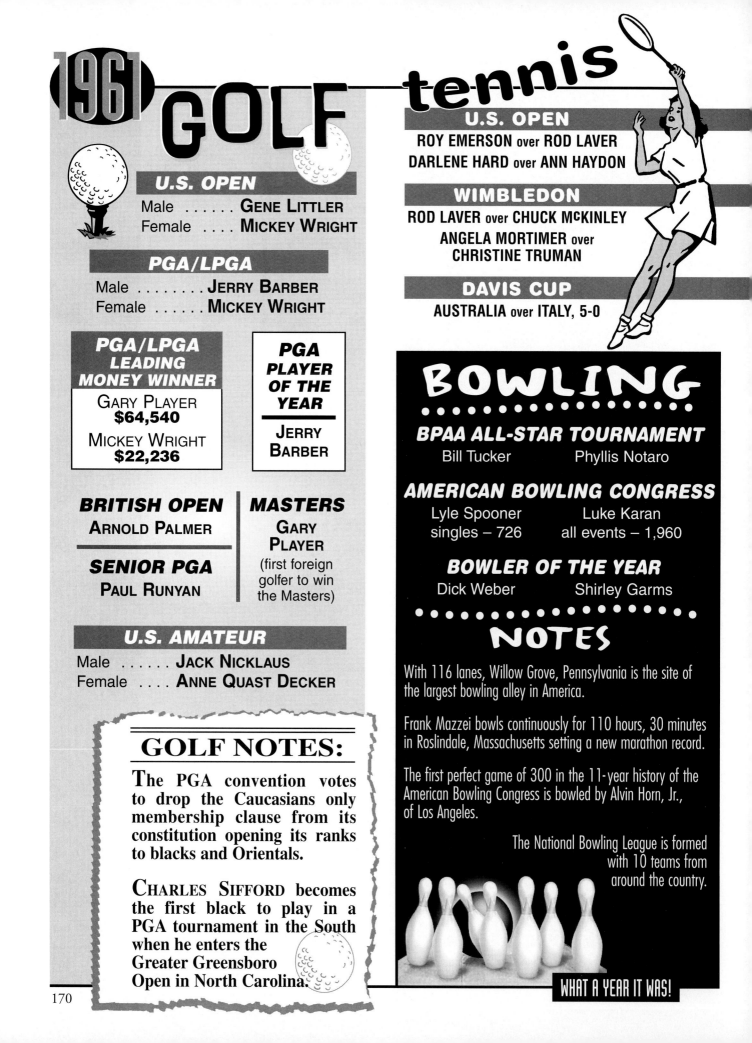

1961 GOLF

U.S. OPEN

Male . . . . . . GENE LITTLER
Female . . . . MICKEY WRIGHT

PGA/LPGA

Male . . . . JERRY BARBER
Female . . . . . MICKEY WRIGHT

PGA/LPGA LEADING MONEY WINNER	PGA PLAYER OF THE YEAR
GARY PLAYER $64,540 MICKEY WRIGHT $22,236	JERRY BARBER

BRITISH OPEN ARNOLD PALMER SENIOR PGA PAUL RUNYAN	MASTERS GARY PLAYER (first foreign golfer to win the Masters)

U.S. AMATEUR

Male . . . . . . JACK NICKLAUS
Female . . . . ANNE QUAST DECKER

GOLF NOTES:

The PGA convention votes to drop the Caucasians only membership clause from its constitution opening its ranks to blacks and Orientals.

CHARLES SIFFORD becomes the first black to play in a PGA tournament in the South when he enters the Greater Greensboro Open in North Carolina.

tennis

U.S. OPEN

ROY EMERSON over ROD LAVER
DARLENE HARD over ANN HAYDON

WIMBLEDON

ROD LAVER over CHUCK MCKINLEY

ANGELA MORTIMER over CHRISTINE TRUMAN

DAVIS CUP

AUSTRALIA over ITALY, 5-0

BOWLING

BPAA ALL-STAR TOURNAMENT

Bill Tucker   Phyllis Notaro

AMERICAN BOWLING CONGRESS

Lyle Spooner   Luke Karan
singles – 726   all events – 1,960

BOWLER OF THE YEAR

Dick Weber   Shirley Garms

NOTES

With 116 lanes, Willow Grove, Pennsylvania is the site of the largest bowling alley in America.

Frank Mazzei bowls continuously for 110 hours, 30 minutes in Roslindale, Massachusetts setting a new marathon record.

The first perfect game of 300 in the 11-year history of the American Bowling Congress is bowled by Alvin Horn, Jr., of Los Angeles.

The National Bowling League is formed with 10 teams from around the country.

WHAT A YEAR IT WAS!

BOXING

HEAVYWEIGHT
Floyd Patterson

MIDDLEWEIGHT
Paul Pender
Terry Downes

WELTERWEIGHT
Benny "Kid" Paret
Emile Griffith

FEATHERWEIGHT
Davey Moore

LIGHTWEIGHT
Joe Brown

LIGHT HEAVYWEIGHT
Archie Moore

Underworld boxing boss FRANKIE CARBO is sentenced to 25 years in prison for trying to take a piece of the earnings of former welterweight boxing champion Don Jordan.

Cycling

TOUR de FRANCE
JACQUES ANQUETIL, France
(wins for the second time)

Near Lahr, Germany, French florist Jose Meiffret pedals his bike at a record-breaking average speed of 109.6 mph for one kilometer breaking his own previous record of 109.05 mph set ten years ago.

At Madison Square Garden, Oscar Plattner and Armin von Buren of Switzerland win the first 6-day bicycle race held since World War II.

Figure Skating

U.S. CHAMPIONS
Bradley Lord
Laurence Owen

SKATING NOTE:
February 15th: The world is shocked by the loss of the entire U.S. figure skating team in an airplane crash in Belgium including champions **BRADLEY LORD** and **LAURENCE OWEN**.

- Passing -

Considered the finest player in baseball history, "Georgia Peach" **TY COBB** dies at age 74 from cancer. In the Major Leagues for 24 years, he was the first player inducted into the Baseball Hall of Fame. Many of his records remain unbeaten including batting average (.367), stolen bases (892), most games played (3,033) and most batting championships (12).

1961

Famous Births

NADIA COMANECI

WAYNE GRETZKY

GREG LeMOND

CARL LEWIS

DON MATTINGLY

ISIAH THOMAS

DENNIS RODMAN

REGGIE WHITE

STEVE YOUNG

SPORT

ASSORTED AWARDS

JAMES E. SULLIVAN MEMORIAL AWARD
WILMA RUDOLPH, *TRACK*
(she sets women's record of 0:11.2 in 100-meter dash)

AP ATHLETE OF THE YEAR
ROGER MARIS, *BASEBALL*

WILMA RUDOLPH, *TRACK*

THE HICKOCK BELT
ROGER MARIS, *BASEBALL*

CHESS

WORLD CHESS CHAMPION
MIKHAIL BOTVINNIK, USSR

U.S. CHAMPION
BOBBY FISCHER*
EVA ARONSON
Bobby wins for the fourth time

DOG SHOW

WESTMINSTER KENNEL CLUB

Cappoquin Little Sister,
Toy Poodle
Florence Michelson, *owner*

WHAT A YEAR IT WAS!

Swimming

ANTONIO ABERTONDO swims the English Channel nonstop both ways staying in the water approximately 43 hours – longer than any other channel swimmer.

1961
track + field

BOSTON MARATHON
EINO OKSANEN, Finland

"The fastest man alive," **FRANK BUDD** of Villanova University, runs 100 yards in a world-record time of 9.2 seconds breaking the record held by Mel Patton since 1948 of 9.3 seconds.

RALPH BOSTON breaks his own indoor broad jump record leaping 27 feet, 1-3/4 inches.

RAFER JOHNSON is one of the first athletes to step forward when President Kennedy announces the formation of a Peace Corps.

CAR RACING

INDIANAPOLIS 500
A.J. FOYT
Bowes Seal Fast Special, **139.131 mph**

LE MANS
OLIVER GENDEBIEN & PHIL HILL
Ferrari 250, **115.88 mph**

DAYTONA BEACH
MARVIN PANCH sets world record in 500-mile race averaging over **150 mph**

WINSTON CUP CHAMPION
NED JARRETT

ITALIAN GRAND PRIX WORLD DRIVERS' CHAMPIONSHIP
PHIL HILL of Santa Monica, California wins the race after his teammate Wolfgang von Trips dies in an accident along with 15 spectators.

FISHING

In Fernandina Beach, Florida Lynn Joyner catches a 680-pound giant sea bass.

"The sad fact is that it looks more and more as if our national sport is not playing at all – but watching. We have become more and more, not a nation of athletes, but a nation of spectators...."

President John F. Kennedy,
December 5, 1961

WHAT A YEAR IT WAS!

1961 WAS A GREAT YEAR, BUT...

THE BEST IS YET TO COME!